Daniel Defoe

Twayne's English Authors Series

Bertram H. Davis, Editor

Florida State University

TEAS 453

Laudatur et Alget
Juven. Sat. I.

DANIEL DEFOE
from the frontispiece to _Jure Divino_, 1706

Daniel Defoe

By John J. Richetti

University of Pennsylvania

Twayne Publishers
A Division of G. K. Hall & Co. • Boston

Daniel Defoe

John J. Richetti

Copyright 1987 by G.K. Hall & Co.
All rights reserved.
Published by Twayne Publishers
A Division of G. K. Hall & Co.
70 Lincoln Street
Boston, Massachusetts 02111

Copyediting supervised by Lewis DeSimone
Book production by Janet Zietowski
Book design by Barbara Anderson

Typeset in 11 pt Garamond
by Williams Press, Inc., Albany, New York

Printed on permanent/durable acid-free paper
and bound in the United States of America

Library of Congress Cataloging-in-Publication Data

Richetti, John J.
  Daniel Defoe.

  (Twayne's English authors series)
  Bibliography: p.
  Includes index.
  1. Defoe, Daniel, 1661?–1731—Criticism and
interpretation.   I. Title.   II. Series.
PR3407.R48   1987   823'.5   87–8550
ISBN 0–8057–6955–2 (alk. paper)

Contents

About the Author

John Richetti is professor of English at the University of Pennsylvania, and has also taught at Rutgers, Columbia and Stanford Universities. He has held fellowships from the Guggenheim Foundation and the American Council of Learned Societies. Among his publications are *Popular Fiction before Richardson: Narrative Patterns 1700–1739* (Oxford, 1969), *Defoe's Narratives: Situations and Structures* (Oxford, 1975), and *Philosophical Writing: Locke, Berkeley, Hume* (Harvard, 1983).

Preface

In the last twenty years or so, a great deal has been written about Defoe's novels, especially *Robinson Crusoe, Moll Flanders,* and *Roxana.* Except for children's editions of *Robinson Crusoe,* however, Defoe is no longer a popular author. He is read now mainly by students of the development of the English novel, for he is generally recognized as an important realistic innovator. Recent critics, however, have refined the traditional view that Defoe was simply a careless journalist who happened to write a couple of books with touches of narrative originality. Increasingly, attention has been paid to Defoe's complicated career as a political and moral writer as well as a producer of popular narratives. Critics have found Defoe's wide experience of the world of his time reflected in his novels and have tried to show how they are self-consciously arranged dramatizations of his ideas about human nature and society. Moreover, some scholars have lately challenged the view of Defoe as an essentially secular writer, who paid lip service to religion but whose novels invite readers to identify with characters who are bent on survival in the economic jungle of the early modern world. Some critics now insist that the novels grew out of the Puritan tradition, that Defoe's fictional autobiographers are best understood as sinners trying to repent and to comprehend the role of divine Providence in their lives. Defoe himself, these critics now persuasively contend, was a skilled impersonator and creator of characters who invite readers to judge their moral failings in the context of the Christian scheme of things.

Defoe has been taken seriously in other ways, too, and critics are still arguing about just how carefully he managed his narrative effects. Debate still rages, for example, about whether or not readers are meant to regard morally inconsistent characters like Moll Flanders with corrective irony. Are Defoe's novels artlessly winning impersonations of adventurers, con artists, thieves, and courtesans? Or are they studies of self-deluded individuals who dramatize their moral bankruptcy and spiritual emptiness? For some critics, Defoe's narratives are original precisely because they raise but do not answer such questions. From this perspective, his fictional autobiographers are uniquely modern selves who dramatize the modern problem of personal identity, simultaneously revealing themselves and concealing their essential natures.

I have tried in this book to do justice to Defoe as a serious creator of morally complex fiction. But I have also attempted to balance this view against the facts of Defoe's career as an exceedingly busy professional author, writing as he himself put it "for bread." Defoe's novels are the most interesting items he wrote, but they are also only a small part of his accomplishment as a writer; therefore, I have devoted a good part of this book to presenting Defoe's nonfictional works, his political and moral journalism especially. I have treated the nonfiction both as essential background for understanding the fiction and as important in its own right. Defoe is, without question, one of the great journalists of his time, a writer of marvelous fertility and incredible range. This book aims to give the reader new to Defoe's work a sense of his immense and inventive fecundity but also to provide a clear guide to the inconsistencies and contradictions his work expresses. The richness and perennial appeal of Defoe's work, fiction and nonfiction, are I believe best understood by taking this balanced view.

John J. Richetti

University of Pennsylvania

Chronology

1660	Daniel Defoe born in London, son of James Foe, a tallow chandler and butcher.
ca. 1671–1679	Attends school of the Rev. James Fisher at Dorking, Surrey, and then Dissenting Academy of the Rev. Charles Morton, Newington Green, north of London.
ca. 1683	Established as a hosiery merchant in London.
1684	Marries Mary Tuffley, with a dowry of thirty-seven hundred pounds.
1685	Fights briefly in rebellion led by the Duke of Monmouth.
1685–1692	Active as a wholesale merchant in the hosiery trade but also deals in tobacco, wine, and other goods. Travels extensively on business in Europe and in England.
1688	Supports the revolution against James II by joining the forces of William of Orange as they march to London.
1692	First bankruptcy, for seventeen thousand pounds.
1694	Establishes a brick and tile factory in Essex.
1697	*An Essay upon Projects,* his first book-length work.
1697–1701	A political agent for William III in England and Scotland.
1701	*The True-Born Englishman,* his most popular poem.
1702	Death of William and accession of Queen Anne. Publishes *The Shortest Way with the Dissenters,* satiric pamphlet on High Church extremists.
1703	Arrested for *The Shortest Way* and made to stand in the pillory. Released through the influence of Robert Harley, Tory minister under Queen Anne. Failure of brick and tile factory and his second bankruptcy.

Chapter One

Daniel Defoe:
A Life of Wonders

There is little hint of Daniel Defoe's future as a writer in his origins and childhood. When he was born in 1660 in the parish of St. Giles Cripplegate, just north of the old city of London, his father, James Foe, was a butcher and tallow chandler (candle merchant), who seems to have become increasingly prosperous during his son's early years. Not much is known about those years, but a few facts are important. Defoe's mother died when he was ten or eleven. He was sent to school in Surrey, south of London at Dorking, and when he turned sixteen, to an academy at Newington Green, just north of London, run by the Rev. Charles Morton. Nonmembers of the Church of England (the Foes were Presbyterians) were barred from the universities at Oxford and Cambridge, and Morton's academy and some others provided alternative education for the sons of prosperous Dissenters who were intended mainly for the ministry. Morton himself was a former scholar of Wadham College, Oxford, with keen interest in modern subjects like science and mathematics. Unlike the traditional course of studies at the universities, which were centered on Greek and Latin, Morton's curriculum stressed modern science and philosophy as well as the proper use of the English language. This last was probably the most significant aspect of Defoe's education. As he recalled years later, Morton "had a class for eloquence, and his pupils declaim'd weekly in the English tongue, made orations, and wrote epistles twice every week upon such subjects as he prescrib'd for them or upon such as they themselves chose to write upon." Morton's writing exercises without doubt helped lay the groundwork for Defoe's future accomplishments as a writer capable of many voices and multiple personalities. "Sometimes they were ambassadors or agents abroad at foreign courts, and wrote accounts of their negotiations and recepcion in foreign Courts directed to the Secretary of State and sometimes to the sovereign himself. Some times they were Ministers of State, Secretaries and Commissioners at home, and wrote orders and instructions to the ministers abroad, as by order of the King in Council and the like."[1]

To be sure, Morton's school was small, some fifty pupils, and lacked the intellectual resources of the universities. Years later, Defoe recalled the disadvantages of "private academies" with some bitterness, noting their lack of libraries and "polite conversation." With such limitations, it was possible for young men of "extraordinary genius, strong parts and great application" to make their way, but "they do not come up to the rate of the first."[2] In later life, as a merchant turned journalist, Defoe was still defensive about his lack of a standard university education and depicted himself as more truly educated by his wide experience and natural curiosity than any student bred in the schools. "Will nothing make a man a scholar but Latin and Greek?" he asked sarcastically in *The Compleat English Gentleman,* a book he was working on when he died. There he describes real learning as the knowledge of history and modern foreign languages, along with a mastery of practical sciences such as geography and astronomy that make one familiar with the actual world. Wittily turning against them the jibes of his enemies that he was a "hosier," Defoe calls the ordinary university graduate of his day "a Greek and Latin monger," who deals "in words and syllables as haberdashers deal in small ware."[3]

Behind Defoe's defiant independence, one detects a lingering feeling of marginality and a sense of his alienating distance from the centers of power. Such resentment is an important feature of Defoe's personality and a recurring, nearly obsessive theme in his writing, a negative force accompanying his enormous energy and omnivorous appetite for ideas and action. Defoe's biographers have conjectured that his youthful intellectual arrogance led to a crisis of faith, turning him away from the ministry for which he seems to have been preparing at Morton's academy. As he wrote some years later of himself, "the pulpit is none of my office. It was my disaster first to be set apart for, and then to be set apart from, the honour of that sacred employ."[4]

After three years at Morton's, his formal education was over. In 1680, as the partner of two brothers, Samuel and James Stancliffe, he was a hose-factor, a middleman between manufacturers and retailers in the stocking or general haberdashery trade. He also dealt extensively in wine and tobacco and other merchandise. During the mid-1680s, he probably traveled widely in Europe on business, acquiring the knowledge of languages and of geography that he put to good use in his later writings. In 1684 he married the daughter of a well-to-do merchant who brought him the substantial dowry of thirty-seven hundred pounds. Although Mary Tuffley bore Defoe eight children, two boys and six girls, little is known of her and the quality or importance of Defoe's domestic life. Much more is certain about his involvement in the political upheavals of the time.

In June 1685 the Duke of Monmouth led an abortive rebellion against his uncle, the new and unpopular Catholic king James II. In his own words, Defoe was "in arms under the Duke of Monmouth," but the actual extent of his participation in the brief struggle is unknown. The rebel forces were completely destroyed in a battle at Sedgemoor and Monmouth was executed on 15 July. Three of Charles Morton's pupils from Newington Green were among the rebels captured and executed, but there is no record of Defoe's prosecution. In March 1686 a general pardon was issued. Defoe may have already sought exile, with many other English sympathetic to the rebellion, in Holland. His most recent biographer notes that the name of Daniel Foe was included in a pardon issued on 31 May 1687 for thirty-three persons "engaged in the late rebellion."[5]

During the 1680s and early 1690s, business and politics were the two interwoven strands in Defoe's life. Legal records indicate that he was involved in a number of suits, no less than eight of them including charges that Defoe had committed fraud. These were litigious times, and Defoe's legal entanglements were not that unusual for an ambitious young merchant. From the beginning, his business dealings appear to have been on a grand scale. One recent biographer wonders just where he acquired the capital and the experience to begin so early and ambitiously. What is clear is that he played for high stakes and probably ventured beyond the limits his capital justified.[6] His dealings included speculating in land and breeding civet cats for their valuable secretions, which were used for making perfume. But various severe losses of cargo at sea during the war with France proved ruinous, and in 1692 all that ambition collapsed in bankruptcy. Defoe owed his creditors the enormous sum of seventeen thousand pounds.

Some distraction from his complicated dealings was surely provided by the civil war of 1688–90 in which James II was deposed. Years later Defoe recalled his proximity to these exciting events. He was at Windsor during the triumphant arrival of the new king William III from Holland in December 1688, and he rode to Henley "where the Prince of Orange, with the second line of his army, entered that very afternoon."[7] As an enthusiastic supporter of the new king, one of the members of a volunteer royal regiment made up largely of Dissenter merchants, he took part in the Lord Mayor's Day parade in 1689, which escorted William and Queen Mary from their palace at Whitehall. As the unfriendly contemporary historian, John Oldmixon, recorded it, among these "gallantly mounted and richly accoutred" troopers was "Daniel Foe, at that time a hosier in Freeman's Yard; the same who afterwards was pilloried."[8]

After his bankruptcy, Defoe managed to survive partly by odd jobs acquired through his political connections. From 1695 to 1699, for example, he was appointed accountant for the government duty on glass ware and bottles, and in 1695 and 1696 he was one of the trustees of the government lottery. These posts brought in only a little money, but through them Defoe may have become known to those in power, to the Whig leaders of the government and eventually to William himself. There are indications that during these years he began to be a secret agent, traveling on business but gathering domestic political intelligence as well.[9] By 1697 or so he had paid a good many of his debts, mainly through a flourishing brick and roof tile factory begun in 1694 in the marsh lands near Tilbury, east of London on the Thames. The factory employed a hundred men, and Defoe later claimed that he generally made six hundred pounds a year profit from it. Such affluence enabled him to buy a new house and set himself up with a coach and horses, a sign of great prosperity.[10]

In the late 1690s, as well, Defoe emerged as a writer. *An Essay upon Projects* (1697) was his first real book and one of the few he openly acknowledged by signing it "D. F." But his energies were chiefly expended in political writing, beginning in 1698 with his first important pamphlet, *An Argument, showing that a Standing Army, with Consent of Parliament, is not Inconsistent with a Free Government*, written to support William's attempt to raise a large army to prepare for the renewed war with France he expected. Other aggressive pamphlets in defense of William's policies followed (for example, *The Two Great Questions Consider'd. I. What the French King Will Do, with Respect to the Spanish Monarchy. II. What Measures the English ought to Take* [1700]), but Defoe's greatest success as William's defender came in a poem, *The True-Born Englishman* (1701), provoked by an anti-Dutch satire by John Tutchin, *The Foreigners*. Defoe described Tutchin's poem as "a vile abhor'd Pamphlet, in very ill Verse" in which the author "fell personally upon the King himself, and then upon the *Dutch* Nation."[11] Pointing satirically to the waves of foreign conquerors from whom England's noblest families, in effect, were descended, Defoe's poem ridiculed English chauvinism and resentment of the Dutch William.

> These are the Heroes that despise the *Dutch,*
> And rail at new-come Foreigners so much;
> Forgetting that themselves are all deriv'd
> From the most Scoundrel Race that ever liv'd.
> A horrid Medly of Thieves and Drones,
> Who ransack'd Kingdoms, and dispeopl'd Towns.
> The *Pict* and Painted *Britain,* Treach'rous *Scot,*
> By Hunger, Theft, and Rapine, hither brought.
> *Norwegian* Pirates, Buccaneering *Danes,*
> Whose Red-hair'd Offspring ev'ry where remains.
> Who join'd with *Norman-French,* compound the Breed
> From whence your *True-Born Englishman* proceed.[12]

Defoe later claimed that the first edition of this phenomenally successful poem sold more than eighty thousand copies. In the first half of the eighteenth century, there were more than fifty editions, making Defoe perhaps the most popular poet of his age. And for the next few years, Defoe was identified in the public mind as the author of this poem. When in 1703 and 1705 he published two collections of his writings, they needed no other identification: *A True Collection of the Writings of the Author of the True Born English-man.*

Defoe also claimed that his poem brought him the personal attention of the king. Whatever their actual relationship, until William's death in 1702, Defoe was in effect a propagandist for his government, defending in various tracts and poems the king's foreign policy of containing the expansionist ambitions of Louis XIV of France. He served, as Frank Ellis suggests, as a sort of semiofficial court poet for the king.[13] Such defense was needed. Many of the English thought William's policies subordinated their interests to Holland's. The parliamentary elections of 1701 returned a Tory majority that stoutly opposed William's policies. As Louis seized the fortresses that lay between France and Holland, fear of further French aggression swept through England. Five freeholders (i.e., men who owned property) from the county of Kent presented a petition to the House of Commons urging it to honor the king's requests for supplies to counter the French. Seeing this as a Whig trick, the House imprisoned the petitioners.

By his own account in a pamphlet called *The History of the Kentish Petition,* this was Defoe's finest hour. Guarded, he tells us, by "16

Gentlemen of Quality, who if any notice had been taken of him, were ready to have carried him off by Force," he presented to the Speaker of the House, "Legion's Memorial to the House of Commons," a protest against the summary treatment of the petitioners and a ringing declaration of an Englishman's civil rights: *"Gentlemen,* You have your duty laid before you, which 'tis hoped you will think of; but if you continue to neglect it, you may expect to be treated according to the resentments of an *injur'd Nation, for Englishmen* are no more to be slaves to *Parliaments,* than to a King. *Our Name is Legion, and we are Many."*[14]

William's death in 1702 unleashed, however, a rising tide of opinion hostile to the Dissenters, who many felt had enjoyed his special protection. One of the key controversies was a proposal to abolish the practice of "occasional conformity" whereby a Dissenter could satisfy the legal requirement for public office of membership in the Church of England by taking communion once a year, continuing to attend his own church the rest of the time. The fires of popular sentiment were fanned by the sermons of Dr. Henry Sacheverell, a Tory High Church extremist whose urgings to "hang out the bloody flag and banner of defiance" formed the background against which in 1702 Parliament considered a bill to prevent occasional conformity.[15]

Defoe's position was ambiguous, for in several pamphlets, notably *An Enquiry into the Occasional Conformity of Dissenters in Cases of Parliament,* he had attacked the practice. He repeated his arguments in 1702 in *The Opinion of a Known Dissenter,* but suddenly on 1 December 1702 he published a pamphlet that marked a turning point in his career. *The Shortest Way with the Dissenters* is Defoe's best-known pamphlet, intended in its outrageous proposals to be a parody of Tory extremism like Sacheverell's. "Now," the pamphlet concludes rabidly, *"let us Crucifie the Thieves.* Let her Foundations be establish'd upon the Destruction of her Enemies: The Doors of Mercy being always open to the returning Part of the deluded People: let the Obstinate be rul'd with the Rod of Iron."[16] The government was not amused, and on 2 January 1703 the Earl of Nottingham, a secretary of state, issued a warrant for Defoe's arrest. Taken into custody that same day, Defoe escaped, and a reward of fifty pounds was offered on the eleventh and again on the fourteenth in the *London Gazette,* the latter valuable for posterity because it features a physical description of Defoe: "He is a middle-sized man, about forty years old, of a brown complexion, and dark-brown coloured hair, but wears a wig; a hooked nose, a sharp chin, grey eyes, and a large mole near his mouth."[17] Desperate, Defoe wrote to Nottingham and from hiding pleaded for mercy: "My Lord a body unfit to bear the hardships of a prison, and a mind impatient of confinement, have been the only reasons of withdrawing myself. And my Lord the cries of a numerous ruin'd family, the prospect of a long banishment from my native country, and the hopes of her majesty's mercy, moves me to throw myself at her majesty's feet, and to entreat your Lordship's intercession."[18]

But Nottingham was adamant. Betrayed by an informer for the fifty-pound reward, Defoe was arrested in May and charged with writing a seditious pamphlet. On the advice of his lawyer, Defoe pleaded guilty, "a sacrifice [as he described it later] for writing against the rage and madness of that High party, and in the service of the Dissenters. What justice I met with, and above all what mercy, is too well known to need a repetition."[19] In spite of intercessions from the Quaker William Penn and Defoe's willingness to tell all he knew, the punishment was unusually severe: sentenced to stand three times in the pillory, pay a fine of 200 marks (about 135 pounds), and serve an indefinite jail sentence. The pillory involved more than the public humiliation and discomfort of standing in the stocks all day. Defoe had angered the Dissenters as well with his pamphlet, and he had reason to fear injury as he stood in the pillory from missiles thrown by a hostile mob.

But Defoe had become a hero for many, and the mob acclaimed him, with cheers and flowers instead of the insults, rocks, and rotten vegetables often hurled at criminals in the stocks. Doubtless, some of Defoe's friends and sympathizers in high places helped keep unruly elements away from the pillory. Defoe himself had helped mold public opinion, publishing while he was in prison a poem (hawked in the street around the pillory as he stood in it, says one tradition), "A Hymn to the Pillory," in which he struck a pose of heroic defiance to state tyranny:

> Hail! *Hi'roglyphick* State *Machin*,
> Contriv'd to Punish Fancy in:
> Men that are Men, in thee can feel no Pain,
> And all thy *Insignificants* Disdain.
>
> . . . .
>
> Thou *Bug-bear* of the Law stand up and speak,
> Thy long Misconstru'd Silence break,

Tell us who 'tis upon *thy Ridge* stands there,
   So full of Fault, and yet so void of Fear;
   And from the Paper in his Hat,
Let all Mankind be told for what:
Tell them 'twas because he was too bold,
And told those Truths, which shou'd not ha' been told.
   Extoll the Justice of the Land,
Who punish what they will not understand.
   Tell them he stands Exalted there
   For speaking what we wou'd not hear.[20]

But there was also mercy in store for Defoe. Through the influence of Robert Harley, the Speaker of the House of Commons, a pardon was obtained from the Lord Treasurer, Sidney Godolphin, who was ordered by Queen Anne to pay Defoe's fine and court costs and to relieve his family. Relief was badly needed, since he had been in Newgate prison for six months and in that time his brick and tile factory had failed and his debts, which he had reduced to five thousand pounds, soared to over eight thousand as he became bankrupt once more.[21] From 1704 onward, when his career as a writer really began, Defoe was continually in debt, harassed by creditors and sometimes living at the edge of financial ruin, precariously supporting himself and his family by writing and by operating as a political secret agent.

While still a fugitive from justice, Defoe had asked his friend William Paterson (one of the founders of the Bank of England) to approach Harley for help, and it was the Tory politician for whom the Whig Defoe became a secret agent. Clearly, Defoe felt that his own had deserted him. The Dissenters, he wrote to Paterson, "like Casca to Caesar lift up the first dagger at me: I confess it makes me reflect on the whole body of the Dissenters with something of contempt more than usual, and gives me the more regret that I suffer for such a people."[22] Owing his freedom to Harley, Defoe offered his services, and in his letters from these months we can see that Harley the moderate Tory, essentially a political pragmatist, had found a useful tool and kindred spirit. Defoe eagerly offered advice, ready to assist Harley with his life's ambition: "How shall you make yourself prime minister of state, unenvy'd and unmolested, be neither address'd against by Parliament, intreagu'd against by partyes, or murmur'd at by the mob—?"[23]

In this remarkable letter or memorandum of July-August 1704, Defoe set forth a detailed plan for Harley's political future, counseling him about the necessity of what today we call public relations ("A man can never be great that is not popular, especially in England"), recommending a certain "dissimulation," a virtuous hypocrisy Defoe calls it, "not unlike what the Apostle says of himself; becoming all things to all men, that he might gain some," and suggesting that a kind of secret service be established to keep the government reliably informed of public opinion.[24] Apparently, Harley was impressed by Defoe's shrewdness, and in the summer of 1704 sent him off to gather information, to set about establishing just such a network of agents.

For the next couple of years, Defoe traveled widely for Harley, on horseback as a private citizen, under assumed names, gathering political intelligence and a stock of knowledge about the economic state of the nation. In September 1706 his destination in these travels was Scotland, where there was opposition to the proposed union of the two kingdoms whereby the Scots would lose their parliament, which would merge with England's. Defoe's tasks were to promote the union, to report efforts to undermine it, to answer, in conversation or in print, arguments against it. This last, of course, had become Defoe's specialty. During King William's time, his reputation as an effective polemicist had been firmly established, and now in Queen Anne's reign his ease and fluency as a writer had no parallel in the history of English political journalism.

In February 1704 he published the first eight-page number of *A Weekly Review of the Affairs of France, Purged from the Errors and Partiality of News-Writers and Petty Statesmen of all Sides*. Shortened to a half sheet of four pages, the *Review*, as it quickly became known, appeared three times a week for the next seven years and consisted mainly of political commentary, but Defoe often ranged widely over history, economics, and the social and moral issues of the day. Produced single-handedly even while he traveled widely as Harley's secret agent, the *Review* has proved invaluable for understanding Defoe's mind and sensibility. Even then, however, some wondered how Defoe could manage alone, and when he was in Scotland reports had it that someone else was producing the *Review*. Defoe responded, obviously proud of his facility, "that wherever the author may be, the papers are wrote with his own hand, and the originals may be seen at the printers."[25]

As James Sutherland remarks, the *Review* was "on many important issues the mouthpiece of the moderate Tory government, a mixture of the official line and Defoe's own varied and independent mind."[26] In addition to the *Review*, Defoe produced a steady stream of other journalism, including key political pamphlets, several considerable poems

(including the book-length verse treatise on government, *Jure Divino*
[1706]), and a number of substantial volumes: *The Consolidator* (1705),
a satirical political allegory; *The History of the Union* (1709), on the
union between England and Scotland; and *An Essay upon Public Credit*
and *An Essay upon Loans* (1710). Included in the shorter journalism
are two important innovative works, *The Storm* (1704) and *A True
Relation of the Apparition of One Mrs. Veal* (1706).

In January 1708 Harley was forced out of office, but Defoe continued
to serve the Tories by working for his successor, Godolphin, until 1710
when Harley returned to office as Lord Treasurer. All this service, for
both men, was entirely secret. Nominally, Defoe was still a Whig, but
his affiliations were apparent. The *Review* was attacked by Whig
journalists, and Defoe branded a turncoat. In 1710 he claimed as always
to be a moderate, caught in the crossfire between extremists: "All the
world will bear me witness it is not a Tory paper. The rage with which
I am daily treated by that party will testify for me. Nay the Tories
will honestly own that they disown it. Yet, because I cannot run the
length that some of the others would have me, *new scandals fill their
mouths,* and now they report I am gone over to the new ministry."[27]
In fact, Defoe was in constant touch with Harley. In 1711 the new
ministry's attempts to end the long-running war with France were
vigorously supported in the *Review* as well as in pamphlets Defoe
published anonymously, such as *Reasons Why This Nation Ought to Put
a Speedy End to This Expensive War.* In all this controversy, which
continued for most of his career, Defoe thrived on his enemies' hostility.

Perhaps the most controversial political issue of these years was the
question of the royal succession. Queen Anne was childless, and by the
terms of the Act of Settlement that accompanied the expulsion of James
II the crown would pass to the Protestant house of Hanover, in Germany,
rather than to the Pretender, the queen's brother, James, the head of
the Catholic house of Stuart in exile in France. As their Whig opponents
charged, Defoe's Tory employers were in fact secretly negotiating with
the Stuarts, even though the cunning Harley kept his contacts open
with the Hanoverians as well. Just how much Defoe knew of these
negotiations is uncertain, but he certainly defended the ministry against
Whig accusations: "For any man to suggest that the new ministry can
be for the Pretender is to me such an absurdity, that saving the duty
of respect to their persons, they must be all mad-men, quite demented
and bereaved, no more fit to hold the reins of the administration in
this nation than a Chinese, or an Indian king."[28]

Matters came to a head in the spring of 1713 when Defoe published three pamphlets in quick succession. Briskly polemical and to some extent ironical tracts, they led, as their titles may indicate, to misunderstanding, ignorant or willful: *Reasons against the Succession of the House of Hanover; And What If the Pretender Should Come? Or, Some Considerations of the Advantages and Real Consequences of the Pretender's Possessing the Crown of Great Britain,* and *An Answer to a Question that Nobody thinks of, viz. But What If the Queen Should Die?* Once again, irony proved disastrous for Defoe. Seizing the long awaited opportunity, Defoe's Whig enemies closed in. William Benson, Thomas Burnet, and George Ridpath, three Whig journalists, made formal complaint to the Lord Chief Justice Thomas Parker. Defoe was arrested and taken to Newgate prison on 11 April 1713. Harley quickly arranged his release on bail, but when Defoe in the *Review* criticized Justice Parker he found himself in jail again for libel. His only recourse was a pardon from the queen, which the ministry obtained on the twentieth of November.

An invaluable propagandist, Defoe needed to be less visible to serve the government well. The *Review* had ceased in the middle of 1713, and he was engaged to write, anonymously, for a periodical called the *Mercator,* which appeared twice a week for about a year. The *Mercator* defended the government's policy of free trade with France, a policy Defoe consistently supported in the *Review* and continued to defend in his other economic writings. His integrity in this regard is hardly at issue, and his complaint in the defense he wrote of himself, *An Appeal to Honour and Justice* (1715), that he was singled out for persecution and abuse by his enemies, has some merit. But when Harley was removed from office in 1714 and when Queen Anne died the same year and the Tories fell from power, Defoe's necessity became great.

His biographers are not certain of Defoe's activities in the years immediately after Queen Anne's death. Familiar troubles recur: he was arrested for a libel on the Earl of Anglesey and convicted in 1715, even though sentence was never passed. He may also have been seriously ill. *An Appeal to Honor and Justice* ends with a publisher's note that while the pamphlet was at the press "the author was seiz'd with a violent fit of an apoplexy," prevented from finishing his defense and "continuing now for above six weeks in a weak and languishing condition, neither able to go on, or likely to recover."[29] If he had been stricken, illness obviously did not affect his literary production, for in 1715 he published the over four-hundred-page first part of *The Family Instructor,* a very popular collection of edifying moral dialogues among members of a family. Indeed, Defoe's literary career was just beginning at the age of fifty-five, and during the next fifteen years or so until his death he wrote the majority of the works for which he is most remembered.

But even as he branched out as a writer to moral and didactic works, pious, even puritanical writings, Defoe remained essentially pragmatic, a political operative who sought to live by serving those in power. In 1714–15 he published in three parts a pseudofictional defense of the embattled Harley, *The Secret History of the White Staff*. But as early as 1715, with the Tory ministry ousted in disgrace, Henry St. John, Lord Bolingbroke, the secretary of state, fled to France and with Harley imprisoned in the Tower of London on charges of treason, Defoe found himself working for the new Whig government and for Robert Walpole, the First Lord of the Treasury and for the next twenty-five years the most powerful politician in England. Defoe's job was to act as a sort of mole within the journalistic apparatus of the Tory opposition, to weaken Tory propaganda from within and to keep the government fully informed. For the next fifteen years, until a year before his death, Defoe was actively engaged in this work as a secret agent, a subversive contributor to a number of Tory journals, notably the influential *Mist's Weekly Journal*. The secret was well kept, not emerging until the discovery of some letters in the mid-nineteenth century, and Defoe in those years was the frequent target of Whig abuse in rival journals.

In the *Review* Defoe made no claim to provide daily news, considering himself an essayist much beyond mere reporting. That lofty position gave way in the face of economic necessity, and much of the journalism that occupied him after 1716 involved reporting events as they happened. In *Mercurius Politicus* (1716–20) and *Mercurius Britannicus* (1718–19), he assembled a monthly digest of news. In *Mist's Journal* (1717–24) and the *White-Hall Evening Post* (1718–20), he discussed these events in more detail. After his disastrous experiences, Defoe seems to have become more cautious. In 1718, for example, he ironically warned the proprietor of *Mist's Journal* that there are ways to survive as a political journalist: speak, he says, "of guilty, great ones ironically,—of the crimes of rulers emblematically, and in all cases relate matters of fact warily. Above most things, speak cautiously of judges and courts of justice,— but above all things, have a care of parliaments."[30]

In April 1719 a final phase of Defoe's career opens with the publication of *The Life and Strange Surprizing Adventures of Robinson Crusoe*, followed a few months later with a sequel, *The Farther Adventures*.

Defoe remained the secret agent and political journalist, writing during 1720–26 for *Applebee's Original Weekly Journal,* to which he contributed, among other pieces on politics and foreign affairs, a series of popular criminal biographies. But he also produced during these years a remarkable series of longer narrative works for which his previous career hardly prepares us: *Memoirs of a Cavalier, Captain Singleton* (1720), *Moll Flanders, A Journal of the Plague Year, Colonel Jack* (1722), *A New Voyage Round the World, A General History of the Pyrates, Roxana* (1724), and *A Tour thro' the Whole Island of Great Britain* (three volumes, 1724, 1725, 1726). In addition, during the prolific last decade of his life he wrote a number of lengthy works on varied topics, including *Religious Courtship* (1722), *The Complete English Tradesman* (two volumes, 1725–27), *The Political History of the Devil* (1726), *Conjugal Lewdness; or Matrimonial Whoredom. A Treatise concerning the Use and Abuse of the Marriage Bed, An Essay on the History and Reality of Apparitions* (1727), *A Plan of the English Commerce* (1728), and *The Compleat English Gentleman* (1729).

Exactly how much Defoe wrote is uncertain, since most of the works scholars attribute to him are unsigned. As a political writer, he necessarily cultivated secrecy, sometimes going out of his way to deny authorship of what he had in fact written. In the autobiographical *Appeal to Honour and Justice,* he complained that "every Libel, every Pamphlet, be it ever so foolish, so malicious, so unmannerly, or so dangerous" was laid at his door. "My Name has been hackney'd about the Street by the Hawkers, and about the Coffee-Houses by the Politicians, at such a rate, as no Patience could bear. One Man will swear to the style; another to this or that Expression; another to the Way of Printing; and all so positive, that it is to no Purpose to oppose it."[31] But even by well-informed modern estimates, the total reckoning from such a busy life of writing is staggering: 566 separate works, including substantial writing for twenty-seven periodicals.[32]

Defoe must have been driven to these heights of production by economic necessity. Since his second bankruptcy in 1704, he seems to have lived comfortably but more or less precariously, scrambling to support his family and to maintain a substantial house in Stoke Newington, north of London. Summing up his life in 1712 in the preface to a collected volume of the *Review,* Defoe looked back on that struggle, stressing like the heroes of the novels he was to write the importance in his life of God's providence and his own remarkable resilience: "I know too much of the world to expect good in it; and

I have learnt to value it too little, to be concern'd at the evil; I have gone through a life of wonders, and am the subject of a vast variety of Providences; I have been fed more by miracle than *Elija* when the ravens were his purveyors; I have some time ago summ'd up the scenes of my life in this distich. *No Man has tasted differing Fortunes more, / And Thirteen Times I have been Rich and Poor.*"[33]

In 1730 he seems to have gone into hiding to avoid prosecution for an old debt. When he died in April 1731, he was alone in a London lodging house and not in his suburban house with his family. His last days were troubled as well by domestic unhappiness, as he lamented in a letter in 1730 to his son-in-law, Henry Baker. Daniel Defoe, junior, to whom Defoe probably transferred his property to protect it from his persistent creditors, had betrayed his father, forcing his sisters and "their poor dying mother to beg their bread at his door." In this letter Defoe looks wearily to his end but with a religious faith it is easy to forget he actually possessed, "hastening to the Place where the weary are at Rest, and where the Wicked cease to trouble; be it that the passage is rough and the day stormy, by which way soever He please to bring me to the end of it, I desire to finish life with this temper of soul in all cases: *Te Deum Laudamus.*"[34]

Chapter Two
Defoe the Political Journalist

When Defoe began writing during the late 1690s the population of England and Wales was about five and a half million, with approximately seven hundred thousand inhabitants in the greater London area. With over a tenth of the nation's people, London was the seat of government and the commercial, artistic, literary, and intellectual center of England. Under the aggressive leadership of William III, England was emerging from internal political and religious strife and was in the process of becoming a major power, successfully challenging the expansionist designs of the French both in Europe and in America. After the 1688 expulsion of the Catholic James II, however, domestic instability was considerable and the threat of invasion and civil war very real, with many of the English opposing the new Dutch king William and encouraging the exiled Stuarts, backed by the French, to attempt their reestablishment. Political allegiances were inextricably entwined with fiercely held religious loyalties. Some ultraconservative members of the "High" Church of England tended to favor restoration of the Stuarts, while more moderate or "Low" Church adherents as well as Dissenters supported William and what was called the Protestant Succession. With William's death in 1702, Anne (James's Protestant daughter) became queen, and while she ruled, a semiinvalid much of the time, the question of the royal succession was furiously debated.

As the political scene shifted and the nation with its allies began the long struggle with France for dominance in Europe known as the War of the Spanish Succession, the structure of society and the distribution of power were changing. Traditional landed wealth gave way to some extent to an increasingly powerful commercial economic order that fed on newly developed foreign markets and raw materials from America. An intense, often rowdy debate about the conduct of national and international affairs took place, a good deal of it in print—in pamphlets, poems, and newspapers. Whig and Tory, originally slang terms of abuse, became accepted labels for opposing factions. The Whigs, associated with the commercial interests but including many landed aristocrats, tended to support overseas expansion and the containment of France.

Tories were of various persuasions, the most radical "Jacobites" favoring the restoration of the Stuarts; others were more moderate. The so-called Country (or anticourt) party was especially opposed to the Whigs' war policy, which depended upon taxes levied almost exclusively on land.

Modern English journalism began, in fact, in London during these years partly in response to the needs of an expanding literate audience concerned with the pressing issues that divided the country. The furious contention they aroused signaled great changes taking place in English culture and national identity. Public opinion, somewhat as we know it today, began to be a factor in political life, and various governments made it their business to subsidize journalists to support their policies and attack their opponents. But of the five and a half million inhabitants of England at the time, it is estimated only about seventy or eighty thousand were literate. So even though estimates of circulation figures suggest that the newspaper-buying public tripled in the first half of the century, the readership for the new journalism and the audience that politicians hoped to reach with it was a very small percentage of the population, probably fewer than one person out of twenty nationwide, though somewhat higher in London.[1]

In part, as well, the emergence of journalism was owing to the gradual relaxation and inefficiency of government censorship during the late seventeenth and early eighteenth centuries. By modern democratic standards, there was considerable restraint on publication, and authors and printers were sometimes persecuted for writings the government considered libelous or seditious. Defoe, of course, was arrested twice. In 1719 the printer John Matthews was hanged for treason for publishing the pamphlet *Vox Populi Vox Dei,* which argued that James II's son was the rightful king of England. But the Licensing Act of 1662 by which official machinery existed to prosecute seditious or even heretical printed matter was allowed to lapse by Parliament in 1694, and prosecutions were on an individual, irregular basis, which gave writers a pretty free hand.

Unlike modern newspapers and magazines, this journalism did not provide instant accounts of daily events; news traveled slowly in those days and governments cloaked their workings in secrecy. Defoe's journalism, typical of the time, consists of commentary on current events, advocacy, polemic, prediction, and lessons for his readers in religion, economics, morals, history, and politics. Especially in periodicals like the *Review,* his writing most resembles modern syndicated columns in newspapers and magazines. Defoe's paper constructed an authorial personality by its regular appearance and consistent point of view. And like syndicated columnists, Defoe and his contemporaries depended for much of their appeal upon controversy; they tended to take sides violently and to spend much of their time attacking and counterattacking each other. Most of this writing and much of Defoe's was, naturally, so intensely topical that it is no longer of immediate interest except to historians, to whom it is in fact invaluable. As one historian puts it, "it is possible to base a study of English society in the early eighteenth century almost entirely on the writings of Daniel Defoe."[2] Defoe succeeded almost too well as a journalist; he served his age, reflecting its immediate concerns with such passionate urgency that he neglected to address posterity.

When Defoe published a collected edition of his works (mostly poems) in 1703, he tried in the preface to set himself apart from the political battles of the day: "I cannot pass for an incendiary: Of all the writers of this age, I have, I am satisfied, the most industriously avoided writing with want of temper; and I appeal to what is now publish'd, whether there is not rather a spirit of healing than of sedition runs through the whole collection, one misunderstood article excepted."[3] To some extent, Defoe's position was essentially moderate, as he steered carefully between extreme views and claimed to be above party and faction. Traditionally, Defoe has been classified as a Whig, a staunch supporter of William III and implacable opponent of those conservatives who sought to restore the Stuarts. The most elaborate and generalized exposition of his political views is the book-length poem *Jure Divino* (1706) in which he vigorously denies the divine right of kings to rule, locates the origin of monarchy in fundamental law, and affirms the right to resist kings "who invade their people's liberties." Even as he states his general principles in the preface to the poem, Defoe is careful to insist on the particular fitness of constitutional monarchy for England: "A monarchy according to the present constitution limited by Parliament, and dependent upon law, is not only the best government in the world; but also the best for this nation in particular, most suitable to the genius of the people and the circumstances of the whole body."[4] Above all, Defoe was a realist. His views are informed by practical shrewdness and an understanding of the human motives behind political positions. Thus, he wrote in one of the early numbers of the *Review:* "Interest is the *Apollo* of princes, and indeed all the princes and states of Christendom are now embark'd in a war for interest; liberty and religion is the aim of a few, but interest is the present article."[5] His political writing is spirited and polemical but mostly free of vituperation. As James Sutherland remarks, Defoe took sides but managed "to give an impression of detachment, of examining a question fairly and without prejudice, and of seeking to produce light rather than heat."[6] Claims of perfect impartiality and modest deference to truth are consistent refrains in Defoe's journalism. Here, from the first year of the *Review*, is a representative statement:

The author pretends to no extraordinary gift of instruction. . . . He presumes so much on the convictive invincible power of truth, that he expects it will bear it self up, *and him upon it,* above the waves and storms of all the seas of faction and parties, he may be obliged to steer thro; and if not, he resolves to venture the shipwreck. He doubts not to force, even those people that will not practise what his arguments move to, yet at the same time to confess they are just, and to own the reason of them. How can he that writes nothing but truth offend? Who can be displeased with him, and what hazards can he run? Truth can never break the law, and therefore can never merit punishment.[7]

Such ringing declarations may be a bit too insistent and rhetorically elaborate to be fully convincing, and in the early eighteenth century when there were no organized political parties in the modern sense, everybody claimed to be above party and beyond faction. Defoe's adversaries, in any event, were not persuaded. Swift, for example, found him "so grave, sententious, dogmatical a rogue, that there is no enduring him" and later called him and the author of another political paper "two stupid illiterate scribblers," singling out for special contempt Defoe's "mock authoritative manner."[8] Another of the wits in Swift's circle, John Gay, conceded ironically that Defoe "had excellent parts, but wanted a small foundation of learning . . . a lively instance of those wits, who as an ingenious author [Swift] says, will endure but one skimming."[9] Defoe had other enemies, but these criticisms are especially significant.

Although he continued nearly to the end of his life to dabble in business, Defoe was a professional author who wrote, as he acknowledged, for money. Necessarily, he wrote hastily if efficiently. "Defoe has a great deal of Wit," said Lord Halifax, one of the great Whig lords whom he served, to the Duchess of Marlborough, and "would write very well if his necessity's did not make him in too much haste to correct."[10] But for some of his opponents, Defoe was merely one of a growing number of ill-educated, poorly paid hacks, Grub Street writers, as they came to be called. As Samuel Johnson defined it in his 1755 dictionary, Grub Street was "originally the name of a street near Moorfields in London, much inhabited by writers of small histories, dictionaries, and temporary poems, whence any mean production is called *grubstreet*." Pope, Swift, Gay, Addison, and other writers of the time depended on literature for their careers and identities; Pope made a substantial fortune with his translations of the Homeric poems, Addison acquired political office, and Swift tremendous political influence through writing. But they did not think of themselves as writing directly for money. Although their work was often topical and polemical, they spoke for the most part to an audience they imagined as select and sophisticated, one able to enjoy classical allusion and ironic complexity, and committed to traditional, deeply conservative notions about human nature and the social order. To use some terms from the intellectual debates of the day, Pope and Swift and their friends were "Ancients" who looked back to classical antiquity for their literary models and tended to disparage the present as culturally inferior. Defoe was a "Modern," for whom the classical past was so much dead lumber, and the exciting present was full of promise and economic possibility. In their gloomier moments, Pope and Swift saw writers like Defoe as symptomatic of the decline of traditional moral-literary values in the face of an undiscriminating popular culture served by pens for hire, the comically degraded characters of Pope's brilliant mock-epic poem, *The Dunciad*. "Restless Daniel," as Pope called him, represented a crude energy, a vigorous but undiscriminating activist optimism that appealed to the unlettered many rather than the exquisite few.

In just that spirit, Defoe's first book, *An Essay upon Projects* (1697), celebrates the possibilities of the present age, initiating his characteristic tone and emphasis and introducing the subjects that he was to address for the next thirty years. In the idiom of the day, a project was a scheme of improvement or invention, and Defoe calls the present "the Projecting Age": "it is, I think, no injury to say, the past ages have never come up to the degree of projecting and inventing, as it refers to matters of negoce, and methods of civil polity, which we see this age arriv'd to."[11] "Negoce" is business, and this book introduces the new hero of Defoe's new age: the merchant.

If industry be in any business rewarded with success, 'tis in the merchandizing part of the world, who indeed may more truly be said to live by their wits than any people whatsoever. All foreign negoce, tho' to some 'tis a plain road by the help of custom, yet it is in its beginning all project, contrivance, and invention. Every new voyage the merchant contrives, is a project; and ships are sent from port to port, as markets and merchandizes differ, by the help of strange and universal intelligence; wherein some are so exquisite, so swift, and so exact, that a merchant sitting at home in his counting-house, at once converses with all parts of the known world. This, and travel, makes a true-bred merchant the most intelligent man in the world, and consequently the most capable, when urg'd by necessity, to contrive new ways to live.[12]

A true-bred merchant himself, Defoe rapidly proposes various improvements: reformation of the banking system, a national tax system for maintaining and improving roads, workers' compensation for merchant sailors and a national social security system, reformation of bankruptcy procedures, a national academy for regulating the English language, a national military academy, an academy for women, and various others. Defoe's vision is rational and nationalistic; he sees England with considerable foresight as the coherent nation-state it was eventually to become, not simply an aggregate of traditional ways and groups but an efficient and rationalized totality. And yet his point of view is empirical rather than visionary. Defoe offers arguments from experience and observed fact: he had been bankrupt and knew firsthand how irrational the law was about debtors; he had traveled England's wretched, ill-maintained roads as a businessman, and as an overseas trader he knew that the merchant marine was crucial to English power.

With remarkable consistency and persistence, Defoe advocated similar schemes for the rest of his life. Both practical man of business and high-minded moralist, he continued to the end of his life to issue proposals to reform and rationalize society. In his otherwise embittered last few years, for example, he published in 1728 an exuberant set of proposals, *Augusta Triumphans: Or the Way to Make London the Most Flourishing City in the Universe*. "I have but a short time to live," he writes, "nor would I waste my remaining thread of life in vain, but having often lamented sundry publick abuses, and many schemes having occur'd to my fancy, which to me carried an air of benefit; I was resolv'd to commit them to paper before my departure."[13] Although such terms were not used then, Defoe was a compulsive critical intellectual, a sort of eighteenth-century version of crankily original figures from our time like Jane Jacobs, Paul Goodman, and Buckminster Fuller.

Defoe seems to have been happiest writing in this wide-ranging, comprehensive manner, but in his work as a journalist day-to-day issues naturally took precedence. And yet even in that journalism, Defoe preserves something of the same critical energy and virtuosity, a fluency, versatility and encyclopedic command of his material that irritated Swift ("so grave, sententious, dogmatical a rogue"). From his earliest pamphlets, Defoe cultivated a deliberate moderation on all issues but also projected a massively informed, richly detailed, and assertive fullness. He generally assumes nothing about his audience, addressing them as if he were a schoolmaster or a preacher. He provides facts and figures almost to excess and seems to enjoy the sheer accumulation of evidence. His first important pamphlet, *An Argument, showing that a Standing Army, with Consent of Parliament, is not Inconsistent with a Free Government* (1698), argues that the House of Commons has the power of the purse and that therefore the king and the army will always be under its control. But he enforces that position by a detailed review of English history stretching back to the Magna Carta.

Something of that same nearly pedantic quality appears in another tract supporting William's policies toward the French. *The Two Great Questions Consider'd. I. What the French King will Do, with Respect to the Spanish Monarchy. II. What Measures the English ought to Take* (1700) is as methodical as its title promises, grounding the argument in Defoe's characteristic psychological realism. Copiously illustrating his point with examples from recent history, Defoe declares that human nature teaches us that "every king in the world would be the universal monarch if he might, and nothing restrains but the power of neighbours."[14] The pamphlet is a lesson in what today we would call geopolitical relationships, since the issue is ultimately economic: "for this I presume to lay down as a fundamental axiom . . . 'tis not the longest sword, but the longest purse that conquers." With effective if somewhat condescending simplicity, Defoe outlines a sequence of inevitabilities in foreign affairs: if the French should get control of Spain and of Spanish America, "they get the greatest trade in the World in their hands; they that have the most trade, will have the most money, and they that have the most money, will have the most ships, the best fleet, and the best armies; and if once the French master us at sea, where are we then?"[15]

In the *Review*, especially, Defoe is bursting with lessons for his audience on every conceivable subject, but in the first few years of its publication his main topic is recent European history. Indefatigably, he outlines the background of threatening French ascendancy and the pressing need to establish a balance of power. Even five years later, as

England and her allies hold out for a total defeat of France rather than
a negotiated peace, Defoe lays the issues out for a public that he clearly
felt needed elementary lessons in foreign policy: "we do not fight against
France as a kingdom, or against the King of *France* as a King, no nor
as a tyrant insulting the liberties of his own subjects; but we fight
against *France* as a kingdom grown too great for her neighbors, and
against the King of *France* as an invader of other nation's rights, and
an oppressor of the common liberties of *Europe*. . . . In short, we fight
to reduce his *Exorbitant Power;* and this consists in that little understood,
but very popular and extensive word, *a Ballance of Power.*"[16] And from
the outset of the *Review,* he complains "that the impatient world cannot
refrain their conclusions, before I am come to mine." Such impatience
is, he concludes, "the effect of writing a history by inches."[17] Fractious
and assertive to a fault, Defoe defies those who resist his instruction.
Some readers, he reports, have found his account of the Swedish war
in Poland too long: "And yet I cannot satisfy my self to close with
this humour of the town, and quit a subject, before I have gone thro'
it, to please the luxuriance of the world's Imagination; such as think
me dull, only because I am long, are like those that don't approve of
the sermon, because they don't love the parson."[18] Few modern readers
will want to work through the material in the *Review* that even some
of Defoe's contemporaries found too circumstantial; yet a good deal of
it is of historical interest. "Mr. Review," as he sometimes referred to
himself, is the first of Defoe's literary mouthpieces, and it is as close
to Defoe himself as a reader will get, outside of his correspondence.

Much of Defoe's effectiveness, in the *Review* and in other political
writing, comes from a cultivated forthright simplicity, a directness Defoe
himself emphasizes as his best quality, even as he implicitly compares
his plain speaking to the clever evasions of other writers. For example,
in a particularly compact number in 1710 he delivers an oration that
both exploits and discards as superfluous the classical parallels other
political writers of the time liked to use. "I could give you similies,
and allegories . . . and read you long lectures upon the *Roman* affairs
under the government of their consuls and tribunes." But he explains
that he prefers "a down-right Plainness, and to speak home both in
Fact and in Stile." As he goes on, Defoe manages to compare the
rejection of the Duke of Marlborough with events from ancient history
but also to insert recent history in a homely sort of way. I could tell
you, he says, about how Sicinius, the people's tribune in Rome raised
the mob against Coriolanus, the savior of the city:

It is as much to the purpose to tell you plainly, how you treat the hero that fights for you, for whose victories you make bonfires, and by whose dangers you triumph! How you raise parties and factions against his honour, reputation, and if it were in your power, *his life too!* As to tell you how the *Athenians* banish'd *Alcibiades,* that had been their generalissimo. . . . It remains then only to put you in mind of the times and things of recent memory: things you need not search your histories for, or ask your fathers about; but may rummage your own memory to confirm.[19]

Mr. Review combines classical eloquence of a sort with everyday remedies summed up in the advice to his audience to "rummage" their memories. But he concludes in this case with fiery exhortations. If you electors of the city of London vote for "madmen for sherrifs," you will "let High Flyers, mad men and Jacobites, have their swinge, that your posts and chains may be pull'd down again, and your streets be adorn'd with gibbets for the execution of those that offer to espouse your liberties."[20] Political pamphleteers tend to claim a monopoly on the truth, and Defoe does it regularly in the *Review* with prophetic intensity. From its earliest days, Defoe dramatizes himself as the embattled, lonely defender of truth in the face of unruly factions; he also calls attention to the difficulty and magnitude of his task in the face of such opposition: "How often have my ears, my hands, and my head, been to be pull'd off,—impotent bullies, that attackt by truth, and their vices storm'd, fill the air with rhodomontades and indecencies, but never shew'd their faces to the resentment truth had a just cause to entertain for them." In spite of "clouds of clamour, cavil, raillery, and Objection," Defoe promises to press on, even though "the field is so large, the design so vast, and the necessary preliminaries so many; that tho' I cannot yet pass for an old man, I must be so if I live to go through with it."[21] As the *Review* went on, even Defoe found himself surprised by his own fecundity. He remarks in the preface to the sixth volume in 1710 that "like a teeming woman, I have thought every volume should be the last—Where it will end now, and when, God only knows, and time only will discover; *as for me,* I know nothing of it."[22]

In its nearly compulsive amplitude, the *Review* exemplifies Defoe's characteristic strength. Committed to nothing less than explaining the history of his time as it unfolds, Defoe pursues historical, political, economic, theological, and moral backgrounds and implications. The more he writes, the more there is to write about. While he forges ahead with this enormous job of explanation and instruction, his subject

expands in range and complexity, as readers and other writers challenge
him and as scenes shift in the great theater of world events. His writing
itself, the *Review* and its enemies and rivals along with Defoe's other
books and pamphlets, becomes part of his subject. Looking back in
1710, Defoe wonders why he does not leave politics (by which he
creates "innumerable enemies on one hand, and very few friends on
the other") and turn to writing "wholly upon matters of trade." But
the rage of party and faction is too strong: "To what purpose should
men talk of trading together, when you can hardly think of living
together?—What commerce can there be, when there is no peace? . . .
This is the thing keeps me so long, from the desireable subject of
trade."²³ To some extent, the paper dramatizes its own heroic feat of
coherent articulation in the face of the political confusion it evokes, just
as it dramatizes its embattled author, somehow in the face of that
chaos preserving his clarity and consistency. These qualities became even
more difficult to sustain after the election of October 1710, when the
Tories held a majority in Parliament and Defoe had to shift his support
of war with France to Harley's plan for a negotiated peace. Defoe's
scrambling through such shifts can be exhilarating if necessarily confusing.
Ordering a great, whirling mass of material and yet preserving something
of its experiential quality as intractable, real confusion, Defoe's style
and sensibility in the *Review* looks forward in this sense to his fictional
characters.

For example, on 1 November 1709 Defoe reports that the *Review*
has had a legal complaint lodged against it as *"A NUSANCE."* Can
it be the government, he wonders, who has begun this prosecution? As
he lists what he has done for the government (and later on in this
paper what he has done for others), Defoe communicates in his repetitions
a delighted self-satisfaction that he has remained steady and purposeful
in a political landscape full of danger and disorder.

Nor can I see any reason to think, this prosecution comes from the government—I am very sure, I have pursued the true Interest of the government,
in prompting the due execution of positive treaties, in setting affairs in a
true light, in detecting the fraud, and pulling off the mask of hypocrites,
who cry'd out of oppression in SCOTLAND, *where there was none;* and calling
that persecution, which was only a just and necessary precaution against the
invasion of *Jacobites.* I have apply'd myself diligently, to appease the *Mur-
murings of the People* against the Government, to open the Eyes of those that
have been impos'd upon by the Enemies of the *Government;* I have wrestled

with doubting Friends and insulting Enemies of *the Government;* I have expos'd my Life to mobbs and tumults, in pressing the nation to unite *under the Government*—and yet am exposing it to the same hazard, in preserving them in that Union *now 'tis made*—I have press'd a peace of parties in *England,* and a peace of nations in *Scotland,* in behalf of, and in obedience to a just and gentle Government.[24]

Energetic, irrepressible, never at a loss for words or solutions to problems, Defoe was almost too persuasive, too forceful for his own good. Some of the most entertaining moments in the *Review* are imaginary dialogues, as Defoe mimics his opponents and other characters on the stage of English political life. Here he imagines a High Church Tory bemoaning the Duke of Marlborough's triumph at Blenheim: "when we come to see all our accounts full of this man's praise, the *Dutch* generals, the *French* prisoners, friends and enemies, all bringing the trophies of the victory to the feet of this unaccountable man, and building altars to his terrible praise, the wound strikes deep, and we see a fatal cloud arising from the smoke of popular incense offered to this idol, which we fear, may in time, spread over the *English* horizon; and being big with thunders, storms, and civil tempests of moderation, may break upon the Church of *England* and overwhelm it."[25] Such mimicry is broadly ironic; it would be obvious even now in someone warning of the danger from "civil tempests of moderation."

Defoe was capable of less extravagant imitation. For example, in *Reasons Why This Nation Ought to Put a Speedy End to This Expensive War* (1711), he had to go out of his way to modify both his voice and his opinions. The *Review* had strongly supported the long war with France. But with the costly victory at Malplaquet in September 1709 in which the French inflicted great losses on the allies, opposition to the Whig war policy grew louder. Written to support the policies of the Tories who took power in 1710, the pamphlet demanded circumspection, since Defoe was paid by Harley to present moderate Whig opinion in the *Review*. As James Sutherland notes, Defoe went to greater lengths than usual here to conceal his identity, since his arguments bore some similarity to those used by Tory pamphleteers.[26] The result is a sober enumeration of the reasons for ending the war, a discussion lacking the fire and invention of the *Review* at its best but quietly eloquent in its opening survey of the results of the long war: "now we see our treasure lost, our funds exhausted, all our publick revenues sold, mortgaged, and anticipated; vast and endless interests entailed upon our posterity, the whole kingdom sold to usury, and an immense treasure turned into an immense debt to pay; we went out full, but are returned empty."[27] Defoe is especially careful not to blame Marlborough and the other generals, targets of violent Tory attacks, for the waste of blood and treasure he outlines so dispassionately. Although Defoe means to be taken completely seriously, the voice here is almost a parody of careful, measured consideration: "It may be therefore a most needful enquiry for the curious heads of this age to reflect back a little upon our own circumstances, and enquire what reasons we have, which are drawn from within ourselves, and turn upon the great hinge of our own affairs only, and which move, and press, and call upon us to put an end to this war upon the best conditions we can."[28] In the context of the brashly assertive, slashing prose of the *Review,* that manner constitutes quite a considerable temporary transformation.

Yet another voice, even more strident than the normally pugnacious Mr. Review, can be heard in *A Seasonable Warning and Caution Against the Insinuations of Papists and Jacobites In Favour of the Pretender. Being a Letter from an Englishman at the Court of Hanover* (1712). Many suspected, correctly we now know, that the Tory ministry was secretly negotiating with the exiled royal family. Defoe's pamphlet briefly denies these allegations, but spends most of its time and achieves its force by two strategies: oratorical fullness and narrative immediacy. Defoe's distinctive strength as a propagandist lies in flashes of narrative, here a brief but vivid picture of subversion: "Every considering protestant cannot but observe with horror what swarms of popish priests from abroad, and jacobite emissaries at home, are spread about among us, and busily employed to carry on these wicked designs; how in disguise they run up and down the counties, mingling themselves in all companies, and in coffee-houses, and private conversation, endeavouring to insinuate with all possible subtlety, favourable notions of the pretender into the minds of the people."[29] Such immediacy is surrounded by the prophetic intensity of Defoe's repeated and inflammatory exhortations to his countrymen. "For God's sake, Britons, what are you doing? And whither are you going? To what dreadful precipices are ye hurrying yourselves? . . . Is this acting like Britons; like Protestants, like lovers of liberty?" This gentleman at the court of Hanover works himself up to a ringing if somewhat vague conclusion: "The work is before you; your deliverance, your safety is in your own hands, and therefore these things are now written: none can give you up; none can betray you but yourselves . . . and if you could see your own happiness, it is entirely in your power, by unanimous, steady adhering to your old principles, to secure your peace for ever. O Jerusalem! Jerusalem!"[30]

Defoe churned out numerous such pamphlets during these tense years, but he seems to have been bored with the easy oratory he devised for his imaginary gentleman from the court of Hanover. *An Answer to a Question that Nobody thinks of, viz. but what If the Queen Should Die?*, written early in 1713, is much more inventive and rhetorically varied. Defoe begins with rough and tumble scatological abuse of his Whig rivals, Abel Roper and George Ridpath, who "have thrown night-dirt at one another so long, and groped into so many jakes's up to their elbows to find it, that they stink now in the nostrils of their own party." At the same time, however, Defoe is a model of good sense, carefully placing himself between extremes, warning against easy answers. Some say the Protestant succession is secure, some say it is in danger, but Defoe offers complexity in place of that opposition. "Both these uncertainties serve to perplex us, and to leave the thing more undetermined than consists with the public ease of the people's minds. . . . Possibly the question propounded may not meet with a categorical answer. But this is certain, it shall show you more directly what is the chief question."[31] But in fact what the pamphlet eventually does is to beat an alarmist drum, to warn that however safe and secure England may be now there will come a time when the crisis will break: "grant this for the present as a fundamental, viz., That we are in no danger of the pretender during this queen's reign, or during this ministry's administration under her majesty; and avoiding all contention of that kind, shall allow our condition to be safe in every article as we go along, for so long as the queen lives, referring the observation of things in every head to those who can answer the main question in our title, viz., But what if the queen should die?"[32] Not only, the pamphlet continues, is the queen mortal but her life is in danger from Jacobite assassins. The initial moderation dissolves into melodrama, drowned out by the drumbeat of Defoe's refrain and by the stark opposition it enforces: with the queen in power we are totally safe from our enemies but when she dies we are totally vulnerable.

In his next two pamphlets in 1713, Defoe tried a much more dangerous gambit. *Reasons against the Succession of the House of Hanover With An Enquiry How Far the Abdication of King James, supposing it to be Legal, ought to affect the Person of the Pretender* is an ironical examination of the advantages England will gain from the Pretender. Given the bickering among parties in Britain, Defoe argues, the Protestant

Succession is bound to fail. Echoing his recurrent complaints in the
Review, Defoe asks how the Elector of Hanover can possibly be supported
once he arrives "while we are in this divided factious condition."[33] But
why not let the Pretender come? Given our hopeless political and
religious divisions, what may well cure us is a violent remedy, a "vomit"
induced by French slavery and popery in the person of the Pretender.
Defoe's metaphor is extended, cumulatively powerful, and yet simple
and homely in style, founded on the proverb he quotes, "desperate
diseases must have desperate remedies."

Now it is very proper to inquire in this case whether the nation is not in
such a state of health at this time, that the coming of the pretender may
not be of absolute necessity, by way of cure of such national distempers
which now afflict us, and that an effectual cure can be wrought no other
way? . . . Even let him come that we may see what slavery means, and
may inquire how the chains of French galleys hang about us, and how easy
wooden shoes are to walk in. . . . If the physicians prescribe a vomit for
the cure of any particular distemper, will the patient complain of being made
sick? No, no; when you begin to be sick, then we say, Oh, that is right,
and then the vomit begins to work; and how shall the island of Britain
spew out all the dregs and filth the public digesture has contracted, if it be
not made sick with some French physic?[34]

   Such a fiery moral metaphor is basically unanswerable. Defoe evokes
British political and religious division so powerfully that he leaves no
alternative to the French purge. Defoe lacked in his ironic pamphlets
the controlling distance that eventually signals the reader to reject or
modify what is actually being said. Such a failure is even more marked
in the next succession pamphlet he wrote in 1713, *And What If the
Pretender Should Come? Or, Some Considerations of the Advantages and
Real Consequences of the Pretender's Possessing the Crown of Great Britain.*
The advantages of the title are, again, almost too convincing at times.
As Peter Earle notes, the irony here has a "measure of truth which
compels attention and even belief." Defoe and much of his audience,
Earle reminds us, would have appreciated "the authoritarian benefits of
French society."[35] What is so bad about French absolutism? asks Defoe's
speaker, pointing again to the hopelessly divided state of the nation.
The absolute rule of the French king makes his subjects "miserable,"
but we are already much more miserable by virtue of our "liberty."

Is not our government miserably weak? Are we not miserably subjected to
the rabbles and mob? Nay, is not the very crown mobbed here every now

and then, into whatever our sovereign lord the people demand? Whereas, on the contrary, we see France entirely united as one man; no virulent scribblers there dare affront the government; no impertinent p——ments there disturb the monarch with their addresses and representations; no superiority of laws restrain the administration; no insolent lawyers talk of the sacred constitution in opposition to the more sacred prerogative. . . . They are all united together so firmly, as if they had but one heart and one mind, and that the king was the soul of the nation: what if they are what we foolishly call slaves to the absolute will of their prince? That slavery to them is mere liberty. They entertain no notion of that foolish thing liberty, which we make so much noise about.[36]

The irony would have been clear enough to any sympathetic reader of the *Review*, who would have learned there that the "constitution" was sacred and royal prerogative was not. Defoe's persona cites the author of the *Review* at the outset of the pamphlet as "that scandalous scribbler" who has tried to tell us that the Pretender will drag us into French slavery.[37] And yet Defoe said he was not surprised when his opponents misunderstood him at first: as he wrote to Harley, "the whiggs (not seeing the satyr upon themselves in it) were all pleased with the book."[38] Defoe's irony needed clearer signals; his narrators in these pamphlets make too good a case. The mimicry is too skilled and the effect too paradoxically convincing for the opposite lessons Defoe hoped to enforce. The result is in fact subversive. The pamphlets, complained the chief justice who had Defoe arrested, contained "arguments to make out that the Pretender has a title to the crown and that the advantages of his reign will be greater than what we now enjoy under her most sacred Majesty (whom God long preserve)." No matter, as he added, that there is in them "a mixture of what they call banter which seems design'd to screen the rest, and to make way for a pretence of an innocent intention." But these, he concluded, are "not subjects to be play'd with."[39]

At their most interesting and irrepressible, Defoe's fullness and exuberance have a subversively playful effect, lending his impersonations a vividness that tends to undercut his satirical intentions. He proudly admitted as much when he looked back in 1705 to the publication of *The Shortest Way with the Dissenters* (1702). To the "High Church Men," he tells us, "the piece in its outward figure, look'd so natural, and was as like a brat of their own begetting, that like two apples, they could not know them asunder."[40] His object, he explained elsewhere, "was to speak in the first person of the party, and then thereby not only speak their language, but make them acknowledge it to be theirs, which they did so openly that [it] confounded all their attempts afterwards to deny it, and to call it a scandal thrown upon them by another."[41] Defoe meant his mimicry, in other words, to slide into accurate and thereby damning imitation of the opinions and preaching style of High Church extremists like Sacheverell. But is there anything in Defoe's tract to tell the reader to reject his speaker's plan to extirpate the dissenters? Or was *The Shortest Way with the Dissenters* ironic only to those who were already disposed against Tory extremism? I think Defoe counted, rather unrealistically as it turned out, on readers rejecting the illogic he placed at the center of the pamphlet's rhetoric, which is foreign to Defoe's own style in his nonironic journalism. That illogic can be summed up in the tract's dependence upon metaphorical violence and an inflammatory biblical allusiveness:

What will ye do for your sister in the day that she shall be spoken for. If ever you will establish the best Christian Church in the world. If ever you will suppress the spirit of enthusiasm. If ever you will free the nation from the viperous brood that have so long suck'd the blood of their mother. If you will leave your posterity free from faction and rebellion, this is the time. This is the time to pull up this heretical weed of sedition that has so long disturb'd the peace of our church, and poisoned the good corn.[42]

Looking back to the toleration of dissenters that led, he says, to the civil war, the speaker exhorts his audience not to be frightened from justice "under the specious pretences, and odious sense of cruelty." To spare future generations, he urges, let us imitate Moses: "a merciful meek man, and yet with what fury did he run thro' the camp, and cut the throats of three and thirty thousand of his dear *Israelites,* that were fallen into idolatry; what was the reason? 'twas mercy to the rest, to make these be examples, to prevent the destruction of the whole army."[43] Exaggeration aside (the Bible says Moses slew only three thousand), this passage marks an interesting shift. From purely metaphorical exhortation, the speaker moves to historical and biblical argument, a parody of the kind of turn Defoe's own polemics take. And when Defoe's speaker goes on to rail against the practice of "occasional conformity" and of small fines for not coming to church, his logic has a paradoxical, disturbing rightness about it: "We hang men for trifles, and banish them for things not worth naming, but an offence against

God and the Church, against the welfare of the world, and the dignity of religion, shall be bought off for 5 s. this is such a shame to a Christian government, that 'tis with regret I transmit it to posterity. If Men sin against God, affront his ordinances, rebell against his Church, and disobey the precepts of their superiors, let them suffer as such capital crimes deserve, so will religion flourish, and this divided nation be once again united."[44]

In an age when religion was still in theory the sustaining moral center of society and in a country where some forms of simple theft were technically capital offenses (punishable by hanging), Defoe's speaker has some justice on his side. In spite of his intentions, *The Shortest Way with the Dissenters* has an incendiary effectiveness. Almost everyone who read the pamphlet took it for genuine. Its spectacular failure as a work of irony tells us a great deal about Defoe's great talent for impersonation, which makes him more than just a competent political journalist. He clearly took a malicious pleasure in mimicry, boasting in a wonderfully revealing moment to Harley in 1706 about his success as a secret agent in Scotland:

I am perfectly unsuspectd as corresponding with anybody in England. I converse with Presbyterian, Episcopall-Dissenter, Papist and Non Juror . . . I talk to everybody in their own way. To the merchants I am about to settle here in trade, building ships &c. With the lawyers I want to purchase a house and land to bring my family & live upon it (God knows where the money is to pay for it). To day I am goeing into partnership with a member of parliament in a glass house, to morrow with another in a salt work. With the Glasgow mutineers I am to be a fish merchant, with the Aberdeen men a woolen and with the Perth and western men a linen manufacturer, and still at the end of all discourse the Union is the essentiall and I am all to every one that I may gain some.[45]

Defoe's concluding allusion is to Saint Paul: "I am made all things to all men, that I might by all means save some" (1 Cor. 9:22). Given the circumstances, the comparison seems outlandish, and yet it is revealing. Defoe liked to compare himself to the apostle. In 1710, for example, he calls his rival authors "of a kind with the creatures, the *Blessed Apostle* engag'd with at *Ephesus*." Like Paul, Defoe confounds his enemies and goads them to fury: "When from the stairs of the castle in *Jerusalem* the Apostle spake to the enrag'd multitude, they stamp'd, fum'd, shouted, and threw dust into the air for madness—

Not able to contradict by reasoning, the force of his words, they bound themselves by an oath to murther him—When he came among the wise, learned *Athenians,* they banter'd and ridicul'd him, call'd him *Ideot,* and *Illiterate,* and their EXAMINERS fell upon him with this, *We will hear what this babler says.*"[46] The self-dramatization is daring enough to make Defoe hesitate ("I am not comparing the *Review* to the Apostle . . . but the rabbles of both times may be compar'd without offence").

On the one hand, Defoe was the shrewdest of journalists, an immensely practical businessman of letters, an adaptable political operative who prided himself on his understanding of human motives, a writer whose prose communicates delight in his powers of persuasion and invention. But on the other hand, Defoe was also steeped in the Scriptures and committed to an uncompromising Christianity. Religious analogies are inevitable for him, even when his situation is thoroughly secular, and preacher and prophet are his recurring modes of self-presentation. Defoe the political writer, the slashing polemicist, can quickly turn to Defoe the moralist reminding his audience of the vanity of earthly glory. When the great Duke of Marlborough died, for example, in 1722, Defoe was led to eloquent musings that cancel his own interest in politics and history:

What then is the work of life? What the business of great men, that pass the stage of this world in seeming triumph, as these men, we call heroes, have done? Is it to grow great in the mouth of fame, and take up many pages in history? Alas! that is no more than making a tale for the reading of posterity, till it turns into fable and romance. . . . Or is their business rather to add virtue and piety to their glory, which alone will pass with them into eternity, and make them truly immortal? What is glory without virtue?[47]

For this Defoe, the world is ultimately governed by a divine plan. Politics and history are thus subordinate to the mysteries of providential design, and the activist individualism and secular optimism of Defoe's economic and political writings have to be balanced against his fundamental belief in traditional religious explanations. Hence the central paradox at the heart of Defoe's personality: he speaks for the new secular age of triumphant British commerce and imperialism, for an expansively assertive individualism, but he is also tied to that Christian world of sin and guilt, of human limitation and divine omnipotence, in which he was raised. An inventive genius and intellectual jack-of-all-trades, he is simultaneously a severe moralist who preaches submission to divine inevitability.

Chapter Three
Defoe as Moralist and Social Observer

More often than not, Defoe's journalism is adversarial. His prose gets much of its slashing energy from his constant readiness to attack. As we have seen, some of his polemics strike at specific opponents, Sacheverell and the High Church Tories, Swift, Tutchin, and other rival journalists. But Defoe has other deliberately less specific targets. Chief among these are what might be called secular and skeptical materialist views of the universe and its workings, which many of Defoe's contemporaries perceived as increasingly popular arguments against traditional religious explanations. At times, Defoe rises to what may strike a modern reader as extravagant estimates of the opposition to religion. For example, when the freethinker John Toland died in 1722, Defoe used his death as an occasion to warn the readers of *Applebee's Journal* "that no age, since the founding and forming the Christian Church in the world, was ever like, (in open avowed atheism, blasphemies, and heresies) to the age we now live in."[1] Threaded through all Defoe's writing is a vigorous defense of Christian cosmology. What makes Defoe's defense of this world view interesting is, once again, his dangerously ambiguous relationship to the positions he attacks, the contradictions with which he flirts between his own implicitly secular outlook and the providential control he quite sincerely aims to uphold.

Even as he sets about in the *Review* to tutor his audience in the history of European realpolitik and to urge it to support strong measures against French domination, Defoe also insists that the historical record demonstrates the regular and numerous interventions of Providence: "The wisdom of Providence is in nothing more conspicuous, than in the frequent expressions of its sovereignty and omnipotence at such seasons, when the designs of furious men would put the creation into convulsions, and carry their projects to a height inconsistent with the honour and majesty of heaven to suffer. In these junctures God is often pleas'd to take the reins of government into his own hands, to check the great monsters of the world in their full career, to make all the nations pay homage to his supreme authority."[2] He wrote that in 1712, when rumours of Louis XIV's death seemed to signal a belated providential deliverance from what Defoe calls a "monstrous reign" of nearly seventy years. Years earlier, even as he analyzed in the *Review* the complexities, political and military, of the War of the Spanish Succession, he declared his objective was "to convince mankind of the secret influence of a supernatural agent." For example, Marlborough's great victory over the French at Ramillies against seemingly overwhelming odds could make sense only as a sign of divine intervention. As usual, Defoe's wonder is balanced by his exact command of numbers and facts, and the victory seems as much the exception or anomaly that proves the statistical rule as an example of God's plan: "To see any army so brave, of such old troops, so numerous, so well prepar'd, so broken, so ruin'd, so entirely overthrown; that of 50,000 men, they can hardly give an account of 15,000; that in less than 10 days, 10 large towns or cities, with above 50 battalions of the Spanish troops, 10,000 deserters, and almost the whole provinces of Brabant and Flanders, should fall into our hands." But here, at least, probability gives way to pious wonder. The astonishing defeats of the French that year are simply things beyond prediction and therefore proof of something other than human control. "Really, gentlemen," says Defoe to those who believe only in natural causes, "this can never be human direction, it must certainly come from God or Devil; choose you whether; you must give it to one of them, and the necessity is remarkable."[3]

As Defoe admitted in the next number, there was no denying that natural causes (such as the lunar eclipse the night King William made his triumphant entrance into London after the peace of Ryswick was signed in 1697) "portend nothing." But he believed that "Providence often directs the times and connections of those otherwise natural causes to concur in such a manner, as may point out to us his meaning, and guide us to understand it."[4] Almost obsessively, Defoe returned to this issue. Five years later, for example, he defended his promotion of a book of prophecies, *British Visions,* which he may have had a hand in writing. Denying that he is one of those "that dream of inspirations, and fancy themselves on the other side of time; that call strong imagination revelation, and every wind of the brain an impulse of the spirit," Defoe yet insists that he knows from his own experience that there are glimpses available of a spiritual world, that there is "a converse of spirits, I mean between those unembodied, and those call'd soul, or encas'd in flesh." Both history and private experience prove the existence

of an "invisible world," and that world confirms "the certainty of
futurity, and above all, the government of Providence, the prescience,
omniscience, and goodness, as well as being of a God."[5] As Rodney
M. Baine summarizes it, in an age when such notions were under attack
and thought to be losing their hold on popular belief, Defoe was "trying
to retain and strengthen all meaningful and credible evidence of Providence, of an invisible world of spirits, and of a communion with
God."[6] And yet Defoe was always very careful, even in his daily
journalism, to avoid dogmatic extremes. For example, in *Applebee's
Journal* in November of 1723 he admitted the probability that comets
"are reserved for the extraordinary errands we speak of *viz.,* that they
are sent as signals of approaching judgments of God upon countries
where they particularly impend." But a month later in the same pages
he was openly skeptical on the same subject, ridiculing popular credulity:
"give me leave to set up against these Doctors who pretend to be
national fortune tellers, and at every portending sign in the event,
supposing any to be portentous, (which however I do not grant,) yet
I say, supposing some may be portentous, I demand whether they
always portend evil, and why not sometimes portend good?"[7]

Defoe's most extended discussion of these matters occurs in three
books he published in the late 1720s: *The Political History of the Devil*
(1726); *A System of Magick; or, A History of the Black Art* (1727);
and *An Essay on the History and Reality of Apparitions* (1727). Fairly
tedious for the most part and often overlapping and repetitive of each
other, these volumes testify by their considerable popularity to the
continuing interest in such questions. It is worth remembering that the
last recorded trial for witchcraft in England was held at Leicester in
1717, the accused being acquitted in spite of twenty-five witnesses who
supported the charge. Even though no one had been hanged for it
since 1685, the act of 1604 making witchcraft a capital offense was
not repealed until 1736.[8] Defoe himself was thoroughly scornful of
popular superstition, and all three treatises on the occult are in part
satires on lingering credulity. All these stories of witchcraft, he comments,
are "so extravagantly wild, that except our hope that most of those
tales happen not to be true, I know not how any one could be easy
to live near a widow after she was five and fifty." Defoe's joke is
deeply meaningful, since the moral reality the devil represents is in fact
often seductively beautiful rather than obviously repulsive. True witches,
he remarks rather wickedly, are not ugly old women but beautiful
temptresses: " 'tis certain the devil has chang'd hands, and that now

he walks about the world cloth'd in beauty, cover'd with the charms of the lovely . . . for who would think a beautiful lady could be a mask to the devil? and that a fine face, a divine shape, a heavenly aspect, should bring the devil in her company, nay, should be herself an apparition, a mere devil?"[9] In all these works on the occult, which seem at first glance to pander to common curiosity about such matters, Defoe in fact heaps ridicule upon the lingering faith in wizards, witches, astrologers, and "cunning men." After telling various stories illustrating their tricks and contrivances, he concludes in *A System of Magick* that modern conjuring is a species of self-delusion: "And here's not an ounce of magic in it all; here's no dealing with the devil in all this. 'Tis nothing but a bite, a kind of a juggle; a devil and no devil, a doctor no conjurer, a vision without a spirit, a dance without a fiddle; and in a word, here was craft, but no knavery either."[10]

For all his piety and polemical scorn for "those modern wits, of which our age is so full . . . who allow no God or Providence, no invisible world, no angelic kind and walking spirits," Defoe's imagination responded enthusiastically to the modern universe of infinite and uni-maginable spaces and innumerable worlds. Even as he insisted that our world actively intersects with a realm of spirits, good as well as evil, his argument is in the end that this hypothesis is simply more rational than other possibilities. His evocation of a spirit world is hedged by qualifications. He can assert only "that there are, or at least may be, a certain number of appointed inhabitants in the vastly-extended abyss of space, a kind of spirits (other than the angels good or bad, and other than the unembodied or uncased souls of men) who dwell in the invisible world, and in the vast no-where of unbounded space, of which we can neither say what it is, what it contains, or how determined."[11]

In the same cautious spirit, Defoe maintains that hell is not a physical location and obviously not the place of burning torture held in popular beliefs, which are "as profane as they are ridiculous." Defoe insists that for anyone who believes in God the existence of the devil is not to be questioned. And yet the devil is a spirit, with all the powers and limitations of that order of being. He cannot assume a human body and he cannot interfere with the natural order of things. In fact, Defoe's devil is simply the archetype of sinful alienation from God, his hell a state of mind into which individuals can easily slip. Defoe defines a "devilish spirit" as essentially a psychological condition, as desires that "form a hell within us, and how imperceptibly they assimilate and transform us into devils, meer human devils, as really devils as Satan himself, or any of his angels." The devil is, to be sure, active in modern times, producing "apparitions and visions of ghosts . . . of which there is so great a variety in the world at this time." But his most effective operation lies not in such delusions but in the psychological effects of evil as they are visibly manifest in history through specific human actors: "thus we have seen a bloody devil in a D'Alva; a profligate devil in a Buckingham; a lying, artful, or politic devil in a Richelieu; a treacherous devil in a Mazarin; a cruel, merciless devil in a Cortez; a debauch'd devil in an Eugene; a conjuring devil in a Luxemburg; and a covetous devil in a M[arlborough]h: In a word, tell me the man, I tell you the spirit that reign'd in him."[12]

Over and over in these three books Defoe's evocation of a supernatural world testifies to the power for him of a world of human compulsion and obsession epitomized in this catalogue of darkly attractive great men. Defoe laughs at most ghosts but speaks movingly of the effects of guilt and forbidden desires, of what he calls "the power of the imagination." "Conscience raises many a devil, that all the magick in the world can't lay; it shows us many an apparition that no other eyes can see, and sets spectres before us with which the devil has no acquaintance; conscience makes ghosts walk, and departed souls appear, when the souls themselves know nothing of it."[13] On the one hand, Defoe warns against self-delusion and "imaginary apparitions" caused by "delirious heads, and the hyppo" [i.e., hypochrondria]; on the other, he conjures up the power of dreams and the terrifying reality of obsessive fantasies. The result is an equation of psychological immediacy and the supernatural: "How is it then that we see in our dreams the very faces and dress of the person we dream of; nay, hear their voices and receive due impressions from what they say . . . tho' we are fast asleep? What secret power of the imagination is able to represent the image of any person to itself, if there was not some appearance, something plac'd in the soul's view, by a secret, but invisible hand, and in an imperceptible manner? which something is in all respects, and to all purposes, as completely an apparition, as if it was plac'd in open sight when the person was awake."[14]

Defoe's explorations of the world of spirits are poised between a traditional, orthodox understanding and a keenly skeptical, empirical sensibility, blunt and forthright. That personality is nicely summed up near the end of *An Essay on the History and Reality of Apparitions:* "let us think of things as they are, not as they are only imagined, and supposed to be; for 'tis the reality of the thing, not the shadow, that can fright and disorder us."[15] A stirring sentence like that seems to put Defoe once and for all in the modern world, far from strange speculations on the occult and the esoteric.

Defoe's most enthusiastic biographer, John Robert Moore, calls him a "citizen of the modern world," and the title is apt up to a point. The England Defoe celebrates in his political and economic writings looks in some ways like the nation that so throughly dominated the world in the nineteenth century. Defoe sounds very often like a propagandist for Britain's expanding future, for the limitless possibilities opened up by trade and technology. Although he was himself a spectacular failure as a businessman, he articulates in his writings a new force and spirit in British life: an ethic of thrift and diligence, of careful commercial accumulation that Defoe saw as the great strength of an expanding middle class, as well as an ambition and entrepreneurial drive that enabled some men of humble origins to achieve great wealth and power. And yet if they are examined carefully, Defoe's views on the economic structure of society are in many ways deeply conservative, even reactionary.

As far as historians can determine, social mobility during Defoe's lifetime was, in fact, minimal. But there were significant social changes under way. During the late seventeenth and early eighteenth centuries, a substantial expansion apparently occurred in the squirearchy and the gentry, that is, of men who held property and power and constituted a substantial ruling elite that increasingly included members of the commercial and professional middle classes. Defoe frequently hails this change in the makeup of the ruling class as an invigorating development. "How are the antient families worn out by time and family misfortunes," he wrote in 1725, "and the estates possess'd by a new race of tradesmen grown up into families of gentry, and establish'd by the immense wealth gain'd, as I may say, behind the counter; that is, in the shop, the warehouse and the compting-house? How are the sons of tradesmen rank'd among the prime of the gentry? How are the daughters of tradesmen at this time adorn'd with the ducal coronets and seen riding in the coaches of the best of the nobility?"[16] Writing in 1709, however, Defoe presented a more balanced picture of society when he estimated that 8 percent of the population belonged to the "gentry, or such who live on estates, and without the mechanism of employment, including the men of letters, such as clergy, lawyers and physicians." By counting farmers, he found that 40 percent of the nation were tradespeople, while about 50 percent constituted "the meer labouring people who

depend upon their hands, such as weavers, butchers, carpenters, shoemakers, labourers, with all kinds of manufacturers, and husband-men,
etc. including apprentices, servants of all sorts, with vagabonds, loiterers,
and unaccountable people."[17] Later that same year, in an essay advocating
population growth as the key to prosperity, Defoe distinguished the
"great" and the "rich" from "the middling people of England, citizens,
shopkeepers, merchants, and gentlemen." These "middle sort of people"
live very well indeed, he says; they "consume the most of any in the
nation," unlike "the poor, that fare hard" and "the miserable, that
really pinch and suffer want."[18]

Although he clearly overestimates the numbers of these comfortable
"middle sort" and underestimates the percentage of the nation that live
by their labor, Defoe's division of society is revealing, reflecting his
experience as a Londoner. His lifetime witnessed the great development
of retail shopkeeping to serve the new commercial wealth that brought
tremendous urban growth and created greatly expanded consumer demand for a new range of luxury goods. The same period also saw a
huge influx of workers to the metropolis from the countryside, a
movement that was continuous because of the high mortality rates in
the city. More people died in London than were born there, and
replacements streamed in steadily to work as servants and in the
manufacturing and service trades the enormous city required.

Along with many other moralists, Defoe was of two minds about
the situation. He recognized that the unprecedented prosperity and the
growing new class of shopkeepers and entrepreneurs he celebrated
depended upon what we now call a consumer society, sustained eco-
nomically by providing, in continually increasing numbers, goods that
are essentially unnecessary. "Our vices," he wrote wittily in 1712, are
"thus made vertues in our trade," and any reformer who would eliminate
"the common vices and luxury of the nation, at the same time begins
the ruin of our trade; and by that time he has brought us to be a
nation of saints will be sure to make us a nation of beggars." With
an informed and detailed breadth of which this extract is typical, Defoe's
vision of the workings of a consumer society expresses his fascination
with this moral paradox: "the fop, the beau, the drunkard, the dancing-
master, are all fellow-labourers in employing the poor, propagating our
manufactures, encrease of commerce, and encouraging navigation: How
many thousand families are daily employ'd by the nameless impertinences
and numberless retinue of the toilet? What fleets at sea, what families
on shoar, what seamen, what innumerable brewing and adulterating,

rabbles of people are employ'd in the manufacture of the bottle and carrying on the wine trade."[19]

Conceding the benefits of such "luxury and extravagancies," he also years earlier lamented "the havock and destruction this custom has made among our ancient nobility and gentry." And yet he notes with some satisfaction how "trade" has "encroached upon nobility and quality." All in all, Defoe describes a restoring social cycle in these matters, and he coolly observes how an aristocracy of money has begun to replace a ruling class ruined by its extravagant way of living. Defoe's hero, the merchant, "stands as fair for a peer as another man, and if wealthy enough, appears every jot as well qualify'd for that dignity." In the same essay, however, Defoe laments the materialism that determines social position: "the world is come to that corruption of judgement now that nothing is more despicable than decay'd quality; and for a man to talk of pedigree and long originals now, without the *addenda* of fortune, equipage, and the *Etceteras* of the family is to make himself the contempt and jest of the company."[20] A man who clearly enjoyed an argument, Defoe is always quite capable of defending contradictory positions, relishing the rhetorical elaboration of different, perhaps equally convincing opinions. In passages that find a famous echo in *Robinson Crusoe,* Defoe amuses himself in the *Review* by apostrophizing money: "Thou art the test of beauty, the judge of ornament, the guide of the fancy, the index of temper, and the pole star of the affections; thou makest homely things fair, old things young, crooked things straight . . . thou makest knaves honest, whores chast, and bullies justices of the peace." But money, he goes on, is a "necessary evil," and earning money is in fact the essentially innocent heart of civilized life: "Subjects honestly labouring, honestly possessing, ought to be left quietly, enjoying what they are masters of; and this is the foundation of what we call law, liberty, and property . . . this is the end of parliaments, constitutions, government and obedience; and this is the true foundation of order in the world, and long may it be our privilege to maintain it."[21]

With an almost obsessive regularity that underlines their seriousness for him, Defoe returns in all his writing to these paradoxes of consumerism. "Trade," he wrote twenty years later in *The Complete English Tradesman,* "is almost universally founded upon crime." Displaying the balanced, unprejudiced view of other cultures he is sometimes capable of, he notes that the Turks, for all their cruelty and barbarity, live without luxuries, simply and therefore honestly. And yet Defoe does not really expect trade to cease; he reasons finally that "the trade does not make the vice, but the vice makes the trade."[22] To be sure, Defoe the bemused observer never cancels entirely the impassioned moralist. But his indignation generally steers clear of the wholesale condemnation of institutions. Instead of locating injustice by the structural analysis of society implicit in his shrewd comments on trade and "luxury," he lights upon corrupt individuals or upon the collective immorality of members of a particular class. One of his earliest pamphlets, *The Poor Man's Plea* (1698), denounces with considerable eloquence the moral irresponsibility of the ruling classes. Calling himself one "of the mob, the poor *Plebeii*," Defoe rails against the bad example and the abuse of power of those in high places: " 'Tis hard, gentlemen, to be punish'd for a crime by a man as guilty as our selves; and that the figure a man makes in the world must be the reason why he shall or shall not be liable to the law: This is really punishing men for being poor, which is no crime at all; as a thief may be said to be hang'd, not for the fact, but for being taken."[23] Six years later, Defoe quoted that very pamphlet and then repeated its radical sentiments: "The punishing vices in the poor which are daily practis'd by the rich seems to me to be setting our constitution with the wrong end upward and making men criminals because they want money." As usual, Defoe varies his moral tone, rising from this fairly dispassionate analysis of injustice to a thundering denunciation of corruption at the center of city government: "Talk no more of well governed cities with aldermen and great folks in them, amongst whom are crimes black as the robes they wear, whose feasts are debauches and drunkenness, whose houses are filled with all manner of excesses, their heads with wine, in their hands is bribery and oppression, and their mouths are full of cursings and blasphemy."[24]

But we must not be misled into seeing Defoe as a champion of the oppressed. This number of the *Review* is part of Defoe's quite intense campaign against a bill proposed by Sir Humphry Mackworth to establish factories to put the poor to work. Convinced that such workhouses would have a disastrous economic effect by competing with private enterprise, Defoe mounted a sustained attack against the bill. He explained his position most fully in *Giving Alms no Charity, And Employing the Poor A Grievance to the Nation* (1704), a pamphlet that exemplifies the admixture of moral and economic notions in Defoe's view of society.

Although he clearly understood that intermittent and seasonal unemployment was built into the economy of his day, Defoe insists that there is plenty of work for everyone. Consider, he argues, the difficulties the army has in recruiting soldiers. If there really were no work, "if the poor wanted employment, if they had not bread to eat, nor knew how to earn it, thousands of young lusty fellows would fly to the pike and musquet and choose to die like men in the face of the enemy rather than lie at home, starve, perish in poverty and distress."[25] The English poor clearly lack that sense of resourceful desperation Defoe later dramatized in his working-class heroes, and he finds them lazy, feckless and improvident: "there's nothing more frequent than for an Englishman to work till he has got his pocket full of money, and then go and be idle, or perhaps drunk, till 'tis all gone and perhaps himself in debt; and ask him in his cups what he intends, he'll tell you honestly, he'll drink as long as it lasts and then go to work for more." An employer himself on a fairly large scale at his brick and tile factory, Defoe claimed to speak from experience. "I affirm of my own knowledge when I have wanted a man for labouring work and offer'd 9s. per week to strouling fellows at my door, they have frequently told me to my face, they could get more a begging."[26]

This self-righteous simplicity seems to have been heartfelt, for in the *Review* of 23 December 1704 Defoe recommended his recently published pamphlet and rose to prophetic intensity on the disastrous social consequences of begging: "the disease is corroded, the leprosie is in the walls; we are possest with the begging-evil." Charity under these circumstances was pernicious on two counts. Not only was it undeserved but it interrupted the system of trade vital to national economic health. Although he sometimes complained about them, Defoe believed in the benefits of high wages as part of a system of exchange and distribution that he consistently evokes by a grand organic image. Workhouses, he argues in *Giving Alms no Charity,* would have a depressing effect on the "inland trade" by producing goods locally that were formerly made elsewhere. "The manufactures of England are happily settled in different corners of the kingdom, from whence they are mutually convey'd by a circulation of trade to London by wholesale, like the blood to the heart, and from thence disperse in lesser quantities to the other parts of the kingdom by retail."[27] So seriously did Defoe take his image of a healthy economic body sustained by the circulation of goods that he consistently opposed industrial improvements that in his view reduced the volume of that vital flow by lessening the number of workers engaged in a particular trade: "All methods to bring our trade to be manag'd by fewer hands than it was before are in themselves pernicious to England in general, as it lessens the employment of the poor, unhinges their hands from the labour, and tends to bring our hands to be superior to our employ."[28] For the same reason, he explains elsewhere, competitive pricing could bring disaster, for "when two of a trade strive to ruin one another by under-selling, it generally ruins the trade and both parties too."[29]

What mattered most for Defoe was the sustaining process inherent in the distribution of goods and services. With its mysterious efficiency, its staggering multiplicity and variety, the market system stirred his imagination and provoked his wonder. In *A Brief State of the Inland or Home Trade of England* (1730), he makes economic process a mercantile version of cosmic order and an allegory of social subordination.

With what admirable skill and dexterity do the proper artists apply to the differing shares or tasks allotted to them, by the nature of their several employments, in forming all the beautiful things which are produced from those differing principles? Through how many hands does every species pass? What a variety of figures do they form? In how many shapes do they appear?—from the brass cannon of 50 to 60 hundred weight, to half an inch of brass wire, called a pin, all equally useful in their place and proportions. On the other hand, how does even the least pin contribute its nameless proportion to the maintenance, profit, and support of every land and every family concerned in those operations, from the copper mine in Africa to the retailer's shop in the country village, however remote?[30]

Such passages from Defoe's work could be easily multiplied. A sort of poet laureate of the market system, Defoe sings, in a sense, the epic of trade and the man, his hero the powerful but benevolent merchant who "sits in his counting-house and converses with all nations and keeps up the most exquisite and extensive part of human society in a universal correspondence." Representing and sustaining the coherence of the world, the merchant testifies, along with the awe-inspiring market system, to nothing less than divine order. God, Defoe explains to the readers of the *Review* in 1706, is plainly visible in the "natural causes" summed up in the commercial structure of that system of trade and distribution:

The generations of the world could not subsist in the manner prescrib'd without the mutual assistance and concurrence of one another. The bare produce of the earth in many of our neighbouring countries could by no means have maintained the numbers of people which the consequences of trade have brought together to answer for this. Navigable rivers, as well as a navigable sea, has made the communication of remote parts practicable; and floaty bodies are adapted for vessels that the light bodies may bear the heavy, and goods that will not bear it may be fenc'd from the inconvenience of weather and preserv'd fit for use and convenience. The rivers and roads are as the veins and arteries that convey wealth, like the blood, to all the parts of the world; and this wealth is the life of kingdoms and towns, the support of their people and test of their power.[31]

Defoe was even more philosophically daring seven years later in the *Review* when he explained that "Providence has adapted nature to trade." God, that is, has arranged the laws of nature so that trade can function, and it is through trade in fact that God most clearly manifests himself. "Shall any tell me that God in his infinite Providence did not guide nations by invisible directions into trade and lead them by the hand into the methods, manner, and consequences to render commerce both easy and useful?"[32]

And yet for all his enthusiasm for a certain kind of economic individualism and the market system it so wonderfully involves, Defoe was in the final analysis an economic conservative to the extent that he consistently opposed alterations in the status quo. What has looked to some of Defoe's critics like innovative theory, Maximillian E. Novak explains, was a deeply conservative "mercantilism" whereby Defoe defended a basically communal ideal of economic activity that favored state regulation of commerce and was fundamentally opposed to what was then emerging as capitalism and its kind of economic individualism.[33] On the whole, Defoe looks back to the early seventeenth century for his economic ideas, evoking in his writings a traditionally hierarchical society, threatened he assures us by the sloth and insubordination of many of the poor, by the ludicrous pretensions of some of the middle classes, by the irresponsible and immoral behavior of the ruling classes, and also it is worth noting by innovators in the world of high finance. In *The Villainy of Stock-Jobbers Detected* (1701), for example, he attacks with special ferocity the speculators who had caused a run on the Bank of England. Such men are worse than marauding armies: "They can draw up their Armies and levy troops, set stock against stock, company against company, alderman against alderman; and the poor passive tradesmen, like the peasant in Flanders, are plundered by both sides and hardly know who hurts them." In place of such wicked subtleties of paper credit, of "the strange and unheard of engines of *interests, discounts, transfers, tallies, debentures, shares, projects,*" Defoe supports "plain trade," "trade upon the square, honesty and industry."[34] Seven years later, in the *Review,* he used nearly the same phrases: "The general commerce of this nation consists of the plain, honest, and downright way of trade, making and manufacturing our wool and other produce of the land, exporting our manufactures and the growth of our country, importing such foreign goods as we want, and circulating our home consumption." Declaring that stockjobbing produces nothing but "knavery," Defoe issues a challenge: "Let any man stand up and tell us what publick benefit the stock-jobbing trade ever brought to this nation." Like the realistic novelist he was to become, immersing his characters in solid objects, in thickly actual transactions and trades, Defoe the economist puts his trust in trade and manufacture rather than in the deluding abstractions of "stocks, tallies, and shares in funds."[35]

Similar moral outrage, not all of it directed at stockjobbers, is threaded through all Defoe's economic journalism. Speculation represented a disruptive force, promising quick wealth for little effort, upsetting traditional patterns of hard work and social order. The threat to that order from the unruly lower classes, Defoe insisted, was equally grave. His concern seems to have reached fever pitch in the mid-1720s in a long treatise, *The Great Law of Subordination consider'd; Or, The Insolence and Unsufferable Behaviour of Servants in England duly enquir'd into* (1724), and in a shorter polemic of 1725, *Every-Body's Business is No-Body's Business; Or Private Abuses, Publick Grievances: Exemplified In the Pride, Insolence, and Exorbitant Wages of Our Women-Servants, Footmen, etc.* The first of these warns that a social crisis exists. Just as the House of Commons has come to dominate the Lords, "so the cannaille of this nation impose laws upon their superiors, and begin not only to be troublesome, but in time may be dangerous; in a word, order is inverted, subordination ceases, and the world seems to stand with the bottom upward."[36] In *Every-Body's Business,* Defoe's persona, "Andrew Moreton," is just as alarmed. He complains that women servants command such high wages and dress so fine that "it is a hard matter now to know the mistress from the maid by their dress, nay very often the maid shall be much the finer of the two." After telling an amusing story of how he was fooled into treating a maid as if she were the mistress of a house he was visiting, he suggests limiting servants' wages and regulating their apparel; otherwise, he warns, social stability will continue to erode. Now, for example, handsome and ambitious servant maids seduce their masters' sons, and "many good families are impoverished and disgrac'd by these pert sluts, who taking the advantage of a young man's simplicity and unruly desires draw many heedless youths, nay, some of good estates into their snares."[37]

As we know from *Moll Flanders,* Defoe was well aware that seduction and betrayal could also work the other way. What is mainly of interest in these shrill polemics is Defoe's (and his projected audience's) attraction to scandalous and shocking narrative and the examples he draws out, sometimes at great length. Like all moralists, Defoe thrives on the sensational details of the transgressions he denounces, and the audience for these tracts was clearly attracted by his skill at spinning them out, drawn probably as much by lurid narrative as by moral indignation. *The Great Law of Subordination* has a rudimentary narrative structure: the narrator is a Frenchman in England writing a series of letters to another Frenchman, describing his adopted country, reviewing its history and surveying its customs, and finding reasons in them for the current chaotic state of affairs. Defoe rehearses his economic theories (wages are too high, the price of corn too low, prosperity in the wool trade has made the laboring poor lazy) and illustrates the dangerous instability in the social structure by telling stories, complete with long stretches of dialogue, about insolent servants.

In one of the most interesting moments, Defoe's narrator describes his infiltration of the unruly counterculture of servants. He has disguised himself "and mingl'd in among the mob of such fellows as those who we call footmen; I have convers'd with them over a mug of porter, as they call their alehouse beer and ale; and there how have I heard them boast over their master's kindness to them, and how they could do anything they pleas'd, that they valued not their masters a shilling, and that they durst not be angry with them; that if they did quarrel, d——n 'em they would be gone, and their master could not do without 'em."[38]

Such vivid particularity and convincing impersonation are crucial features of Defoe's skill as a popular moralist. Almost in spite of his intentions and indeed because of the urgency of his denunciations, Defoe evokes in works like this an authentic urban scene, full of color and lifelike energy. Taken as a whole, his observations on society, dating back to the early days of the *Review* and extending through his many contributions to other periodicals, provide an often vivid panorama of many aspects of life in the early eighteenth century. Such observations also point to the link between Defoe's now little-read didactic works and what we think of as those purely fictional narratives for which he is remembered. Almost from his earliest days as a journalist, Defoe displayed unusual narrative skill, enough to dispel some of the mystery that surrounds his emergence as what we now call a novelist with the publication of *Robinson Crusoe* in 1719 at the age of fifty-nine. The *Review* included what were in effect short stories in the form of letters from (presumably) imaginary correspondents who described complicated dilemmas that read like plot outlines. For example, on 14 April 1705 he discussed a letter asking advice from a woman whose husband had deserted her and who had two suitors ready to propose. More important, however, is the development in the *Review* of Defoe's talent for evoking the texture of contemporary life as he experienced it.

An especially interesting example occurs in the *Review* in 1713, a denunciation of the extravagance infecting some of the shopkeeping merchants he so much admired. Defoe founds his complaint in a vividly rendered anecdote, one he used later to great effect in *Moll Flanders*. Out walking upon business "very late in the city," he encounters a fire "in a citizen's house, in none of the wealthiest part of the town." In a moment profoundly typical of Defoe the curiously detached but meticulously accurate social and moral observer, he finds there is nothing he can do to help and places himself "in a convenient corner near the fire to look on, and indeed the consternation of the poor people was not fruitless of remarks." What strikes him amid the "noise, terrible gestures and distortions" is the nature of the possessions being thrown out a window to save them from the fire and the reactions of one of the victims to the loss of her finery:

Here I saw out of a shopkeeper's house velvet hangings, embroidered chairs, damask curtains, plumes of feathers; and in short, furniture equal to what formerly suffic'd the greatest of our nobility, thrown into a street flowing a foot deep with water and mud, trodden under foot by the crowd and then carried off piece-meal as well as they could. . . . In the house which I stood nearest to, which was opposite to the fire, and was in great danger too, the wind blowing the flame, which was very furious directly into the windows, the woman, or mistress . . . had several small children; her maids, or nurses, or whatever they were, made great diligence to bring the children half naked and asleep, down-stairs in their arms. . . . One of these maids coming again, as if to fetch another, meets her mistress, whose concern, it seems, lay another way, with a great bundle. The mistress screams out to her, "Mary, Mary, take care of my cloaths; carry them away; I'll go fetch the rest." The maid, more concern'd for the children than the mother, cries out louder than her mistress, "Lord, Madam, where's Master Tommy? The child will be burnt in the bed." [She] throws down the cloaths and runs up stairs.

The mistress, whose fine cloaths lay nearer her heart than her child, cries out, "Oh! There's all my cloaths," snatches up the great bundle, and runs out of the house half naked with it and leaves the wench to go fetch her child, who, poor lamb, was almost suffocated with the smoke and heat.[39]

Now, Defoe's moral purpose is not irrelevant here. Vanity and foolish social ambition such as he wants to denounce are at the heart of this vignette, driving out maternal concern in a revealing moment. But Defoe's command of the scenic materials in a few economical narrative strokes is masterful: flames, furniture, mud and water in the street, the noise and confusion, and then the focus on the frenzied, shouted exchange between mistress and maid. One of the problems for modern readers of Defoe is that in his various longer didactic works this same compact fusion of moral purpose and narrative immediacy is rarely present.

A perfect example is *The Family Instructor* (1715, a second volume in 1718), the first part of which is a series of dialogues with interspersed commentary and narrative in which a father and mother awaken to the necessity of religious principles in regulating the life of their family. The catalyst in this conversion is their youngest child, who by a series of innocent queries brings his parents back to a consciousness of their Christian obligations. (For all their solemn didacticism, sequences like this mark very clearly Defoe's fascination with psychological process, with moments of intense self-discovery.) Two of their older children, used to secular pleasures, resist conversion, and the readable parts of the book, inevitably, are their spirited refusals to give up things like riding in the park on Sundays and going to plays. And yet no matter how thickly he lays on the piety, Defoe always seems to do justice to rebellious energy and individual recalcitrance. Deeply interested as a moralist in the roots and causes of behavior, he uses some striking metaphors, one of them distinctively Lockean, to explore the process by which a personality is formed:

Nature, like some vegetables, is malleable when taken green and early; but hard and brittle when condensed by time and age. . . . The temper of a child, misled by vice or mistake, like a dislocated bone, is easy to be reduced into its place, if taken in time; but if suffered to remain in its dislocated position, a callous substance fills up the empty space, and, by neglect, grows equally hard with the bone, and resisting the power of the surgeon's skill, renders the reduction of the joint impossible. . . . Then, as to correction, the heart being hardened as before by opinion and practice . . . the blow of a stripe makes an impression on the heart of a child, as stamping a seal

does on the soft wax, the reproof even of words on the same heart when
grown up, and made hard, is like striking upon steel, which instead of
making an impression on the metal, darts back sparks of fire into your
face.[40]

Those metaphors indicate a fascination with the effects of individual
deviance that often shares the stage in Defoe's didactic works with long
stretches of tediously edifying discourse. Although he tries to repent in
the end, the elder brother's defiance has a consistency and force that
Defoe does not suppress. At moments like this, Defoe sounds like a
playwright, freed from his moralizing responsibilities and out simply to
dramatize unresolvable conflict:

SON: This is intolerable! I had as lieve you would turn me out of your door;
I'll be content to go to the West Indies, or be a foot-soldier, or anything,
rather than be made such a recluse: why was I not bred like a priest? Then
you might have sent me to a monastery, and I might have been used to a
cloister life: but to breed me up for a gentleman, and then confine me as
no gentleman is confined, this is exposing me, and making me look like a
fool among all company! (He flies out in a rage.)
. . . .
SON: I care not what I do, or whither I go. (He walks about in a great
passion.) FATHER: Unhappy, foolish youth! had I extorted obedience to any
unreasonable, unjust thing; had I put you to any hardships, had I exposed
you to any dangers, or deprived you of any lawful pleasures, these things
might have been alleged, and you might have had some pretence of talking
thus to your father. . . . Yet the thing I desire is so just, so reasonable, so
necessary, so much my duty to command, and your interest to obey, that
I cannot, I will not go from it, or abate one tittle of it; and therefore, you
may consider of it, and act as you will; you know my resolution, and fall
back, fall edge, I will have it done, so you make take your choice for God
or the devil. (Father goes out and leaves him.) SON: You may be as resolute
as you will, you will never bring me to your beck. What! must I forsake
all my mirth and good company, and turn hermit in my young days! Not
I, I'll go to the galleys rather, I'll seek my fortune anywhere! Not go to the
park! nor see a play; be as demure as a quaker! and set up for a saint!
What shall I look like? (swears aloud) I won't be a mountebank-convert,
not I; I hate hypocrisy and dissimulation, I have too much honour for it.[41]

In the rebellious career that follows this outburst, Defoe sketches a
scenario for a novel of action and adventure he might well have written:
the son goes abroad without the tutor his father wished, "spends his

estate, gets a commission in the army, is disbanded, comes home a cripple and a beggar; and though always very penitent for rejecting his father's government and instruction, yet never submits himself to his father, so as to be received again, and dies miserable."[42]

As the most extended work Defoe produced in the years immediately preceding the publication of *Robinson Crusoe, The Family Instructor* is an adumbration of some of his main fictional themes. It examines what was then widely felt to be a moral and social crisis, the crumbling as the historian Lawrence Stone says of "the political and religious values that lay behind patriarchy."[43] *The Family Instructor* thus moves on to examine the breakdown of order beyond the immediate family circle and treats rebellious servants and apprentices. Lending a degree of unity to Defoe's interminable dialogues, this crisis of authority naturally proves a resonant theme, allowing Defoe the moralist to move from domestic and personal turmoil to the broadest contemporary social, moral, and theological questions.

Chapter Four
Robinson Crusoe and the Novel of Adventure

Robinson Crusoe

The title pages of Defoe's books tell us a great deal about them. *The Life and Strange Surprizing Adventures of Robinson Crusoe, of York. Mariner: Who lived Eight and Twenty Years, all alone in an un-inhabited Island on the Coast of America, near the Mouth of the Great River of Oroonoque; Having been cast on Shore by Shipwreck, wherein all the Men perished but himself. With An Account how he was at last as strangely deliver'd by Pyrates. Written by Himself.* Whether Defoe or his publisher composed this enticing summary hardly matters, since it identifies the narrative's double attractions. *Robinson Crusoe* was meant both to astonish and to reassure, to combine the fantastic and the familiar, the story at once of unparalleled adventure and domestic routine. The title page is aimed at the substantial audience that existed then for travel literature, for accounts of voyages into a largely unknown world where the exotic and the wonderful tended to be the rule, and where the line between the real and the imaginary was not always clearly drawn. We know, from the sale catalogue of his library, that Defoe himself was an avid reader of travel accounts. But the exact details of time and geography carefully advertised on the title page of *Robinson Crusoe,* which promises personal and authentic narration, make this book much more than exotic adventure.

In *The Rise of the Novel,* Ian Watt has called Defoe's innovation "formal realism." Defoe, says Watt, is perhaps the first writer of fiction to embody the "circumstantial view of life," that is, to present with some degree of success what claims to be the actual, authentic experience of an individual. Till then, narrative had more or less aimed to transform experience, to shape it according to literary and moral tradition, to represent characters and situations that tended to have a general rather than a particular validity. In so far as it was considered valuable, literary

narrative moved away from particular, merely individual reality to the
higher truth available only in the typical. Narrative, as Watt explains,
thus reflected the influence of traditional philosophy, which located truth
in general ideas rather than in particular representations. The emergence
of what we now call the novel is in part a symptom of the philosophy
and psychology that emerged in the seventeenth century in the works
of thinkers like Descartes and Locke, who argued that individual
experience and perception were primary, the foundation of all knowledge.
Defoe's fiction, as Watt says, "is the first which presents us with a
picture both of the individual life in its larger perspective as a historical
process, and in its closer view which shows the process being acted out
against the background of the most ephemeral thoughts and actions."
In Defoe's novels, we have "a sense of personal identity subsisting
through duration and yet being changed by the flow of experience."[1]

In constructing his fiction, of course, Defoe was not immediately
concerned with (or even conscious of) these issues. We cannot say
exactly why he suddenly turned in 1719 to writing long narratives, but
that development is hardly surprising in the career of an enterprising
journalist. By writing the pseudoautobiography of a shipwrecked sailor
surviving on a deserted island, Defoe clearly sensed a profitable opportunity to please a large audience demonstrably eager for the strange
and surprising. The book's success was immediate, so much so that
the critic Charles Gildon was irritated enough to attack it that same
year in *The Life and Strange Surprizing Adventures of Mr. D . . .
DeF . . . of London, Hosier.* In an amusing dialogue, Gildon imagines
Defoe explaining to an outraged Crusoe the sort of popular fame he
has been granted: "there is not an old woman that can go to the price
of it, but buys thy life and adventures and leaves it as a legacy, with
the *Pilgrim's Progress,* the *Practice of Piety,* and *God's Revenge against
Murther,* to her Posterity."[2]

Defoe seems to have found the germ of the story in the life of
Alexander Selkirk, a Scottish sailor who was marooned after a disa-
greement with his captain on the island of Mas a Tierra, largest of
three islands in the Juan Fernandez group, three hundred fifty miles
off the coast of Chile. Selkirk was rescued four and a half years later
and became something of a celebrity when he arrived in London in
1711. Since Defoe is sometimes accused of being simply a sort of
inspired reporter, some of the differences between Selkirk's story and
the life Defoe invented for Crusoe are extremely revealing.

As the captain who rescued him, Woodes Rogers, observed, Selkirk had adapted himself to his wild isolation. When his gunpowder ran out, he hunted goats by running after them, "for his way of living and continual exercise of walking and running, clear'd him of all gross humours, so that he ran with wonderful swiftness thro the woods and up the rocks and hills." To some extent, Selkirk reverted to an appropriately "natural" state, learning to do without salt and bread, living naked for a time and running barefoot through the island as his feet grew hard. When he first came on board Woodes Rogers's ship, "he had so much forgot his language for want of use, that we could scarce understand him, for he seem'd to speak his words by halves."[3] When Richard Steele met him in 1711 in London, Selkirk said that he found consolation for his loneliness on the island in reading the Bible and "grew thoroughly reconciled to his condition," his life turning into "one continual feast, and his being much more joyful than it had before been irksome."[4]

Crusoe's life on the island centers precisely, almost obsessively, on his efforts to avoid Selkirk's plausible adaptation and to maintain civilized ways. Defoe's great accomplishment as an observer of human psychology lies in having Crusoe avoid Selkirk's sweet serenity and in always, sometimes in spite of himself, rendering the profound emotional ambivalence of his solitary hero. And, of course, Defoe invented a whole series of incidents in Crusoe's life that have no parallel whatsoever in Selkirk's otherwise quite ordinary life as a sailor. When Defoe set himself the task of imagining experiences like Selkirk's, he complicated enormously what his simple source provided, transforming it from a tale of survival into a pioneering work of realistic fiction that also turned into a profound cultural parable, at once a story with universal appeal packed with specific spiritual, moral, political, and economic implications.

Defoe was very self-conscious about the spiritual and moral parts. Crusoe insists that his story demonstrates how God saved him physically and spiritually, and how these extraordinary events prove that Providence is at work in the world. Gildon's sneering comparison of *Robinson Crusoe* with popular pious works testifies to Defoe's success in conveying that purpose. To some extent, *Robinson Crusoe* forms part of Defoe's lifelong polemic against secular philosophy. But that religious purpose proved fruitful for Defoe's conception of his character. In fact, much recent scholarship has insisted that Defoe's originality derives from his imitation of the pattern of spiritual autobiography, which licenses Crusoe's extended self-examinations. Evangelical Protestantism encouraged regular spiritual exercises of this sort and recommended keeping journals to record significant religious experiences and feelings. For Puritans like Defoe, grace and salvation were apprehended not by the external rituals or sacraments of a church but by solitary, internal encounters with God. Meditation, aided by the focusing devices of journals and autobiographies, was an essential means to that end. Ostensibly, Crusoe's story is an exercise in religious retrospection; as he meditates on the events of his life, the mature Crusoe is able to see the providential warnings he was blind to as a willful young man, ignoring his father's advice to stay home and be content with his lot. After describing a terrifying storm and shipwreck during his first short sea voyage from Hull, Crusoe reflects on what he should have done. His comparison is significant: "Had I now had the sense to have gone back to Hull, and have gone home, I had been happy, and my father, an emblem of our Blessed Saviour's parable, had even killed the fatted calf for me" (36–37). Pushed on by his desires, for adventure and wealth, the young Crusoe takes no notice of such clear warnings and biblical parallels, even the one his captain subsequently invokes when he tells him that perhaps the wreck itself is a warning from God and Crusoe is "like Jonah in the ship of Tarshish" (37).

As J. Paul Hunter says, *Robinson Crusoe* follows a familiar Christian pattern, which Defoe's original audience would have grasped immediately: disobedience-punishment-repentance. For early eighteenth-century Christian readers, what looks concretely realistic in Defoe's story may well have been inherently metaphorical. They would perhaps have responded primarily to what Hunter calls the "emblematic" nature of Defoe's realism and found Crusoe's isolation meaningful as an epitome of the "Puritan version of the plight of man."[5] And, as individualized and complex as the events of Crusoe's life appear, they clearly follow, as G. A. Starr observes, "a conventional and regular pattern of spiritual evolution."[6] As he gradually turns into a thoughtful Christian during his long solitude, Crusoe looks back on his past life in order to trace his spiritual growth, to find evidence of God's purpose in what would to the uninstructed appear as merely the random events of a life. Like the father in *The Family Instructor,* Crusoe awakens from religious indifference to a sense of heightened awareness, both of himself and of God's role in his fate.

There are, however, crucial differences between the static didacticism of *The Family Instructor* and the dynamic unfolding or shaping of Crusoe's inner life. In his retrospection, pattern and meaning appear fitfully, provoked and surrounded by vividly rendered events, external and internal, that have no real function in Crusoe's spiritual autobiography. That autobiography testifies to the power of the disruptive individuality he says repentance teaches him to renounce. Even as he acknowledges God's hand, Crusoe grows more and more the master of the island and his fate, until by the end of his story he is both cunning and powerful in arranging his escape from it. Crusoe's story is full of wonders but no miraculous interventions. Defoe's great achievement is to make his hero's repentance and religious awakening aspects of a convincing psychological profile; they form part of Crusoe's instinct for survival. For the modern reader, these religious emotions make special sense as an intensely coherent response to the terrors of isolation. The discovery of providential direction and support gives Crusoe peace of mind and allows him to work more efficiently. But thanks to Defoe's narrative gifts, the recreated moments of Crusoe's past are more than parts of the jigsaw puzzle of a guiding Providence; they have a material, nearly palpable immediacy that marks the beginnings of realistic fiction in English.

For an example, consider the "mountain-like" wave that sweeps Crusoe ashore on his island and drowns all his fellow sailors:

Nothing can describe the confusion of thought which I felt when I sunk into the water; for tho I swam very well, yet I could not deliver my self from the waves so as to draw breath, till that wave having driven me, or rather carried me a vast way on towards the shore, and having spent it self, went back, and left me upon the land almost dry, but half-dead with the water I took in. I had so much presence of mind as well as breath left, that seeing my self nearer the main land than I expected, I got upon my feet, and endeavoured to make on towards the land as fast as I could, before another wave should return and take me up again. But I soon found it was impossible to avoid it; for I saw the sea come after me as high as a great hill, and as furious as an enemy which I had no means or strength to contend with; my business was to hold my breath, and raise my self upon the water, if I could; and so by swimming to preserve my breathing and pilot my self towards the shore, if possible; my greatest concern now being, that the sea, as it would carry me a great way towards the shore when it came on, might not carry me back again with it when it came back towards the sea. (64)

Crusoe invokes only briefly the panic he must have felt at that moment, but he records with an eye for the exact sequence of events what he instinctively did. Defoe's sprawling, loosely strung sentences evoke a complicated scene as they chart precisely the turbulent movements of water and waves. Just barely held together with coordinating conjunctions (and, but, for), these sentences also swirl with qualifications, distinctions, and a crucially placed simile ("that wave having driven me, or rather carried me . . . as high as a great hill, and as furious as an enemy"). As Pat Rogers puts it, Defoe's prose in *Robinson Crusoe* manages a fidelity both to the facts and to the *impression* of those facts, pointing by its persistent referentiality to the objects of experience but also by its syntactical looseness and repetitiveness to the subjective effects of experience. "The prose," Rogers says very suggestively, "never gets a firm hold on its materials: the style has a struggle on its hands, just as the hero does."[7] These features of Defoe's prose may be said both to evoke the confusion of the moment and to render it both fully and precisely. The next paragraph continues the scene:

The wave that came upon me again, buried me at once 20 or 30 foot deep in its own body; and I could feel my self carried with a mighty force and swiftness towards the shore a very great way; but I held my breath, and assisted my self to swim still forward with all my might. I was ready to burst with holding my breath, when, as I felt my self rising up, so to my immediate relief, I found my head and hands shoot out above the surface of the water; and tho' it was not two seconds of time that I could keep my self so, yet it relieved me greatly, gave me breath and new courage. I was covered again with water a good while, but not so long but I held it out; and finding the water had quite spent it self, and begun to return, I strook forward against the return of the waves, and felt ground with my feet. I stood still a few moments to recover breath, and till the water went from me, and then took to my heels, and run with what strength I had farther towards the shore. But neither would this deliver me from the fury of the sea, which came pouring in after me again, and twice more I was lifted up by the waves and carried forwards as before, the shore being very flat. (64–65)

Crusoe tries to remember much more than the panic he evokes; his narration preserves a quantified, measurable world. He carefully estimates that he is pulled twenty or thirty feet below the surface of the great wave, and remarks that it is his head and hands only that shoot up above the surface for "not two seconds of time." The reader is invited to imagine a demarcated sequence of images, rather like a set of different frames in a moving picture. Both of these paragraphs point, as well, to the ultimate secret of Crusoe's survival and to the special perspective that enables Defoe's realism. Like a sort of instinctive empirical scientist, Crusoe cooperates with destructive natural forces, exerting himself only when progress forward is possible; in similar fashion, Defoe's narrative defers to the facts, balancing Crusoe's desire for pattern and moral meaning against an objective recording of what he saw and did. Thus, as Crusoe walks on the shore and contemplates his deliverance, he reflects "upon all my comrades that were drowned, and that there should not be one soul saved but my self; for, as for them, I never saw them afterwards, or any sign of them, except three of their hats, one cap, and two shoes that were not fellows" (66). It is hardly an exaggeration to say that this catalogue marks a crucial moment in the development of the novel. That flotsam conjures up the pathos of a world of isolated, unrelated items, of phenomena that defy the human impulse to order by seeming to have no meaning other than their presence. Even as he begins his meditation on the fate that put him on the island, Crusoe brings us reports of that world of mere phenomena, things and events that are real precisely because they have no meaning beyond their random factuality.

As he goes about the business of survival on his island, Crusoe is a meticulous reporter as well as a patient observer and experimenter. But he lacks certain things, notably bread. Thus, he is astonished one day to see barley growing just by his fortified dwelling. Only God, he begins to suspect, could have "miraculously caused this grain to grow without any help of seed sown." He must have arranged it "purely for my sustenance on that wild miserable place" (94). But Crusoe then remembers that he had shaken out over that spot where the barley grows "a bag of chickens' meat." His wonder begins to abate as the force of accident and random event reasserts itself. A mature Crusoe now knows better, as he explains: "I ought to have been as thankful for so strange and unforseen providence, as if it had been miraculous; for it was really the work of providence as to me, that should order or appoint, that 10 or 12 grains of corn should remain unspoiled . . . as if it had dropt from heaven" (95). Providence here works through what appear to be the random events and chances of daily life. Crusoe's world of ordinary things and commonplace events, if viewed correctly, is evidence of an ordering Providence. Thus, years later when Crusoe is cutting wood to make charcoal he discovers the entrance to a cave just as he is wondering how he can continue to make a fire and not be discovered by the cannibals. As he narrates this moment, Crusoe revises its meaning, steering his reader and himself away from what it obviously looks like: "meer accident (I would say, if I did not see abundant reason to ascribe all such things now to providence)" (182). Defoe's realism thus looks for a justification for its close inspection of the material world and seeks to avoid the implications of the randomness it evokes so powerfully.

Not all the facts in *Robinson Crusoe* are quite that random, but the plot, as Watt points out, is totally subordinated to "the patterns of the autobiographical memoir," as Defoe substitutes the sequences of individual experience for the traditional plots of narrative.[8] Defoe deliberately begins with details whose crucial purpose is to ground the tale in actuality and to make Robinson Crusoe an individualized character whose life has historical and geographical particularity: "I was born in the year 1632, in the city of York, of a good family, tho' not of that country, my father being a foreigner of Bremen, who settled first at Hull" (27). And Crusoe's fateful shipwreck is preceded by his career in a number of specifically rendered historical and geographical milieus: after a very profitable share in a voyage to "Guinea" (that is, the coast of western Africa), he is taken prisoner during his next trip by Moorish pirates and spends two years as a slave in Sallee, in North Africa. Escaping from there, he winds up in Brazil as a tobacco planter. Finally, disaster arrives when he and some of his fellow Brazilians set out on an illegal, unlicensed expedition to buy slaves for their plantations (the Spanish monopoly of the slave trade called the *asiento* having made them prohibitively expensive). As one critic suggests, Crusoe's movements make commercial sense in that Defoe sends him from the old and narrow mercantile sphere of the Mediterranean to "the larger circle of the commercial trade world in the seventeenth century."[9] Defoe was too well informed to leave such matters vague, and the plot of *Robinson Crusoe,* however strange and surprising it may become, turns on particularized historical facts.

Indeed, what Crusoe attempts on his island is much more than survival; he tries to duplicate the civilization from which he has been separated and in his dogged way he recapitulates European society's technological transformation of nature. Necessity forces him to seek food and shelter, but cultural habit drives him to try to bake bread, to make furniture, and to fashion pottery so that he can bake and boil. As generations of fascinated readers can testify, his experiments are enthralling; they seem to reenact the trial, error, and accident by which we imagine technological progress has taken place in primitive times.

But even as he busily fashions his environment, Crusoe naturally longs for human contact. Next to the necessarily solitary excitement of his discoveries (and perhaps as their price), he experiences a profound loneliness. When a ship is wrecked on the rocks of the island, Crusoe is devastated to find no survivors. Defoe's rendering of Crusoe's state of mind is especially powerful, since it records his involuntary physical reactions: "I believe I repeated the words, 'O that it had been but one!' a thousand times; and the desires were so moved by it, that when I spoke the words, my hands would clinch together, and my fingers press the palms of my hands, that if I had any soft thing in my hand, it would have crusht it involuntarily; and my teeth in my head wou'd strike together, and set against one another so strong, that for some time I could not part them again" (193). And yet in spite of those emotions, Crusoe's salvage operation is coldly efficient, his inventories thoroughly detailed. Two dead seamen's chests yield "a fine case of bottles, of an extraordinary kind, and filled with cordial waters, fine and very good . . . some very good shirts, which were very welcome to me; and about a dozen and half of linnen white handkerchiefs and coloured neckcloths; the former were also very welcome, being exceeding refreshing to wipe my face in a hot day" (197).

By virtue of his desperate situation, Crusoe rediscovers, in a sense, the fragility of his humanity and realizes how crucially dependent it is upon the tools and artifacts of civilization. "I spent whole hours, I may say whole days, in representing to my self in the most lively colours how I must have acted if I had got nothing out of the ship . . . that I should have lived, if I had not perished, like a meer savage; that if I had killed a goat or a fowl, by any contrivance, I had no way to flea or open them, or part the flesh from the skin and the bowels, or to cut it up; but must gnaw it with my teeth and pull it with my claws like a beast" (141). The imaginative secret of Defoe's book lies in these reflections, as Crusoe vividly pictures the alternative to his achievement, what would have become of him without his tools. For a moment, in place of the sensible and patient master of the island, Crusoe becomes primitive man, an animal with teeth and claws rather than the clean technology of gunpowder and fire. All of Crusoe's arrangements are a struggle against that possibility in himself and, more immediately, against potential enemies who may devour him.

Crusoe's efficiency is spurred on, in short, by emotions that extend from fearful self-loathing to a terror of external enemies. Much of his activity centers on defense not just from the elements but from unknown human rivals. Among the considerations for establishing his dwelling place on the island he lists "security from ravenous creatures, whether men or beasts" (76). What he devises with incredible and protracted labor is nothing less than a fortress. He drives hundreds of sharpened stakes into the ground in front of his tent to form a barrier, weaving ship's cable through them so "that neither man or beast could get into it or over it" (77). Then he begins to burrow into the rocky hillside behind his tent, laboriously carving out a cave, piling the excavated earth and stone to strengthen further his fortress. Similar arrangements surround the "bower" Crusoe builds for himself inland where he gathers grapes and eventually keeps his herds of tamed goats.

Now this paranoia gives way in time to a kind of satisfaction. Crusoe claims in due course that his solitude gives him a contemplative understanding of the world. Alone, he is exempt from the temptations of society and from its morally destructive economic competition and deluding false values. On the island, he necessarily values only that which he can use and the lesson is a profound one: "In a word, the nature and experience of things dictated to me, upon just reflection, that all the good things of this world are no farther good to us than they are for our use; and that whatever we may heap up indeed to give others, we enjoy just as much as we can use and no more" (140). From the first, however, Crusoe is revealingly inconsistent. Finding some gold and silver coins on the wrecked ship, he soliloquizes: " 'O drug!' said I aloud, 'what art thou good for? Thou art not worth to me, no, not the taking off of the ground; one of those knives is worth all this heap; I have no manner of use for thee, e'en remain where thou art, and go to the bottom as a creature whose life is not worth saving.' However, upon second thoughts, I took it away" (75). In the same spirit of realistic inconsistency, Crusoe even as he lives simply and naturally on his island still manages to accumulate a fortune, for his plantation in Brazil has prospered in his absence. Like Job (Crusoe's own comparison), he is materially rewarded for his long suffering, and the miracle of his deliverance is matched by the wonders of compound interest: "I was now master, all on a sudden, of above 5,000£. sterling in money, and had an estate, as I might well call it, in the Brasils, of above a thousand pounds a year, as sure as an estate of lands in England" (280).

From one modern perspective, what drives Crusoe as a young man is thus not just his wanderlust or greed or rebellious rejection of his father's advice. As Watt observes, Crusoe's "original sin" is in fact "the dynamic tendency of capitalism itself, whose aim is never merely to maintain the *status quo,* but to transform it incessantly."[10] Instinctively and inevitably, the character Defoe imagines is, from one point of view, a representative economic individual, defined neither by family ties nor social relationships but by a process of accumulation. As many commentators, including Karl Marx, have noted, Crusoe represents the modern economic individual, transforming nature by assigning value to its products through labor, creating a realm of specifically human worth. In place of financial assets, Crusoe acquires the techniques of survival and the experiences of an incredibly eventful life, but he cashes all that in at last for ready money. In effect, Crusoe's solitary activities allow that process of accumulation to be colorfully human and blameless, a matter of natural survival rather than soulless economic domination.

Even as he uses the island in an enlightened and wholly "natural" way for his survival, Crusoe also appropriates or colonizes it, taking he tells us "secret" pleasure in political posession: "to think that this was all my own, that I was king and lord of all this country indefeasibly, and had a right of possession; and if I could convey it, I might have it in inheritance as compleatly as any lord of a mannor in England" (114). Crusoe's little joke becomes deadly serious later in the book when he kills the cannibals and metes out justice to English mutineers. In part, such sentiments reflect Defoe's strong interest throughout his life in establishing English colonies in South America to challenge Spanish dominance. Back in 1712 he had proposed to Harley that an English colony should be founded in what is now southern Chile and Patagonia. In 1724 he published *A New Voyage Round the World,* in part the story of a detailed and totally imaginary trek across the Andes. That book's purpose was to drum up interest in establishing an English settlement in that part of the world, where Defoe of course had never been but which he pictures as a fertile paradise abounding in gold. Crusoe's sentiments are related to Defoe's colonial propaganda, but they also point to his more generalized resonances as a cultural archetype, a representative of European imperial expansion as it reached out for raw materials and slaves.

Defoe's instinctive acuteness, then, makes Crusoe both historically and psychologically meaningful. His anxiety is part and parcel of his competence as a survivor; he transforms nature but senses that it is still dangerous. He claims to learn nature's lessons but in fact his way of living on the island is defined by imported cultural patterns and political structures. He is master of all he surveys, as the poet William

Cowper later wrote of Selkirk, but he is tormented by loneliness and fear of others. He renders a world of precisely observed natural fact and technological process, but he also evokes a world of nightmares, terrifying obsessions, and deep anxieties. Crusoe's description of the alternations of contentment and despair in his early years on the island catches the complex pathos of his life: "the anguish of my soul at my condition would break out upon me on a sudden, and my very heart would die within me, to think of the woods, the mountains, the desarts I was in; and how I was a prisoner, locked up with the eternal bars and bolts of the ocean, in an uninhabited wilderness, without redemption. In the midst of the greatest composures of my mind, this would break out upon me like a storm, and make me wring my hands and weep like a child" (125).

Defoe devises two solutions to this dreadful ambivalence. One lies in religious introspection. Weak from an illness, Crusoe reads the Bible and finds new meaning in the familiar text "Call on me, and I will deliver you," which he now understands as deliverance from sin rather than literal rescue from his island. This spiritual consciousness is prepared for by Crusoe's balancing of the good and evil aspects of his situation. In double columns, evils are placed against goods: "I am cast upon a horrible desolate island, void of all hope of recovery. But I am alive, and not drowned as all my ship's company was" (83). Reconciliation with God is made possible in effect by Crusoe's increased awareness of the complex relativity of experience, which he expresses in these reassuring commercial metaphors: "there was scarce any condition in the world so miserable, but there was something negative or something positive to be thankful for in it; and let this stand as a direction from the experience of the most miserable of all conditions in the world, that we may always find in it something to comfort ourselves from, and to set in the description of good and evil, on the credit side of the accompt" (84). Crusoe's piety is often tedious but ultimately convincing because Defoe dramatizes it as a crucial means of survival that grows out of his hero's psychological stress at its most extreme.

But eventually there is another, more satisfying solution to Crusoe's precarious mental state, a shift from the personal internal world of survival and self-definition to the external world of adventure and conflict with others. *Robinson Crusoe* seems to turn abruptly from spiritual autobiography into a novel of exciting adventure, although the sudden shift seems at first yet another problem for poor Crusoe's troubled psyche. "It happened one day about noon going towards my boat, I was exceedingly surprized with the print of a man's naked foot on the shore, which was very plain to be seen in the sand" (162). Though he frenziedly searches for others, Crusoe finds just the one foot print and is once more plunged into terrified uncertainty. Even when Crusoe solves the mystery and discovers that cannibals periodically visit his island to eat their prisoners of war, even when he actually sees them at their horrible feasting, the certainty only heightens his anxieties. The transition, in other words, from Crusoe's inner world to the sphere of action is deliberately slow and thereby effectively involving and convincing. For all its absorption in the stable external world, *Robinson Crusoe* views that world through the filters of its narrator's necessarily unstable consciousness. Defoe's special originality lies in never losing sight of that interplay of subjective perception and the external world. Indeed, the traditional account of Defoe as a "realistic" novelist distorts his achievement by overemphasizing the objectivity of his style. As G. A. Starr points out, close examination of his writing reveals that his characters tell us very little in fact about the external world. Instead of being factual or referential, Defoe's style creates a realistic illusion "by ascribing to the object qualities which the narrator comes upon, not through simple observation," but by a process of interpretation whereby "things and events are rendered as perceived, as in some sense transformed and recreated in the image of the narrator."[11]

Paradoxically, the materialization of Crusoe's worst fantasies in the cannibals plunges him into his most intense self-examination. After finding the remnants of their visit, "the shore spread with skulls, hands, feet, and other bones of humane bodies" (172), Crusoe becomes obsessed with their destruction: "night and day I could think of nothing but how I might destroy some of these monsters in their cruel bloody entertainment, and, if possible, save the victim they should bring hither to destroy" (175). If Crusoe has learned anything on his island, however, it is to balance desire against possibility, to wait and see and measure and observe. After a period of internal debate, he decides that it is not for him to judge in these matters. As a thoughtful eighteenth-century traveler, Crusoe arrives at an enlightened anthropological view of the cannibals and their customs: "They think it no more a crime to kill a captive taken in war, than we do to kill an ox; nor to eat humane flesh, than we do to eat mutton" (177).

And yet for all his hard-won restraint, Crusoe is still, he admits, subject to desires he cannot repress. During a sleepless night, he broods on the possibility of escape held out by the cannibals: "it occurred to me to enquire what part of the world these wretches lived in; how far off the coast was from whence they came . . . and why I might not order my self and my business so, that I might be as able to go over thither as they were to come to me" (201). His daring final resolve is crucially significant for Crusoe's mature personality. He decides to try to capture one of the cannibals and to use him as a guide to get to the mainland. "But as I could pitch upon no probable means for it, so I resolved to put my self upon the watch, to see them when they came on shore, and leave the rest to the event, taking such measures as the opportunity should present, let be what would be" (203).

From this point on, Crusoe's island is a busy thoroughfare, visited by cannibals several times and, in the island sequence's last episode, by English mutineers. Throughout these complicated events, Crusoe is true to his formula: he is a detached observer who acts to his advantage as opportunity arises. His strategy is not only effective but wonderfully consistent with the attitude to the world he has perfected on the island. As he makes the transition from solitary survivor to adventurous man of action, Crusoe maintains the same tactics. He is attentive to any sort of possibility, ready to respond swiftly to whatever may happen, modifying his position accordingly. Just as he learned by infinite patience and painstaking observation to make pots, bake bread, tame goats, and so on, now he defers to unpredictable reality and waits for "the event." Crusoe watches the world like a hawk, and when the moment for action arrives his instincts are swift and precisely effective. For example, in the following account of his first battle with the cannibals impulse follows observation but, in Crusoe's narration at least, it is as calmly methodical in execution as the process of observation itself. In part, this is a narrative effect: Crusoe is watching himself in action as he tells his story. But the past tense of the narrative gives way in the face of Defoe's accumulating particulars and active verbs to an intensely present moment. Watching through his telescope, Crusoe sees that one of the prisoners the cannibals have brought this time has broken away and is pursued by three men:

It came now very warmly upon my thoughts, and indeed irresistibly, that now was my time to get me a servant, and perhaps a companion or assistant; and that I was called plainly by Providence to save this poor creature's life; I immediately run down the ladders with all possible expedition, fetched my two guns . . . and getting up again, with the same haste, to the top of the hill, I crossed toward the sea; and having a very short cut, and all down hill, clapped my self in the way between the pursuers and the pursued; hallowing aloud to him that fled, who looking back, was at first perhaps as much frighted at me as at them; but I beckoned with my hand to him to come back; and in the mean time, I slowly advanced towards the two that followed; then rushing at once upon the foremost, I knocked him down with the stock of my piece; I was loath to fire, because I would not have the rest hear; though at that distance it would not have been easily heard, and being out of sight of the smoke too, they wou'd not have easily known what to make of it. Having knocked this fellow down, the other who pursued with him stopped, as if he had been frighted; and I advanced a-pace towards him; but as I came nearer, I perceived presently he had a bow and arrow, and was fitting it to shoot at me; so I was then necessitated to shoot at him first, which I did, and killed him at the first shoot. (206)

The rest of *Robinson Crusoe* is a series of similar triumphs, as Crusoe is transformed from an introspective, cautiously defensive settler to an aggressive adventurer and domineering colonial overlord. The captured cannibal becomes his servant, Friday; Friday's father and a Spaniard, rescued from cannibals three years later, complete the peopling of the island. Once again, Crusoe jokes about his power: "it was a merry reflection which I frequently made, how like a king I looked. First of all, the whole country was my own meer property; so that I had an undoubted right of dominion. 2dly, my people were perfectly subjected: I was absolute lord and lawgiver; they all owed their lives to me, and were ready to lay down their lives, if there had been occasion of it, for me" (240–41). But in fact in what follows Crusoe acts like a king or even like the Providence to which he always defers. Recalcitrant nature and inscrutable Providence give way in this last third or so of the book to a masterful Crusoe, who embodies both these forces as he presides in the very last sequence over a reenactment of his own initial predicament. When he watches from his hiding place as the mutineers prepare to maroon their captives, he draws out the lesson very explicitly:

This put me in mind of the first time when I came on shore, and began to look about me; how I gave my self over for lost; how wildly I looked round me; what dreadful apprehensions I had; and how I lodged in the tree all night for fear of being devoured by wild beasts. As I knew nothing that night of the supply I was to receive by the providential driving of the ship nearer the land, by the storms and tide, by which I have since been so long nourished and supported; so these three desolate men knew nothing how certain of deliverance and supply they were, how near it was to them, and how effectually and really they were in a condition of safety, at the same time that they thought themselves lost and their case desperate. (250)

With considerable flair, Crusoe casts himself in the role of deus ex machina. As he dramatically presents himself to the startled captain and his men, the dialogue points to his transformation into an agent of divine order. " 'He must be sent directly from heaven then,' said one of them very gravely to me, and pulling off his hat at the same time to me, 'for our condition is past the help of man.' 'All help is from heaven, sir,' said I. . . . 'Am I talking to god or man! Is it a real man, or an angel!' 'Be in no fear about that, sir,' said I, 'if God had sent an angel to relieve you, he would have come better cloathed, and armed after another manner than you see me in' " (252–53). And a few pages later as Crusoe's design begins to operate, the captain is apprehensive. "I smiled at him, and told him that men in our circumstances were past the operation of fear" (258).

Pirates in Fact and Fiction

In what follows, Defoe imagines a complicated set of strategies whereby the numerically superior mutineers are subdued by Crusoe and his men. In all his subsequent fiction, Defoe displays a fascination with similar strategies, whether part of the guerrilla tactics of a small group against larger numbers or the shifts and dodges of thieves and confidence men against society. But these events at the end of the island sequence also have a larger significance. Using a combination of firepower and tactical shrewdness, Crusoe in the rest of his story fully and finally embodies that modern Ulysses, the adventurer-explorer. In part, he is a figure who brings order and justice to the wild places of the earth, but he is also the systematic destroyer of native resistance to the European order he represents. James Joyce noticed this aspect of *Robinson Crusoe,* calling it a "prophecy of the empire" and Crusoe a prototype of the British colonist. "The whole Anglo-Saxon spirit is in Crusoe: the manly independence; the unconscious cruelty; the persistence; the slow yet efficient intelligence; the sexual apathy; the practical, well-balanced religiousness; the calculating taciturnity."[12]

In the sequel Defoe quickly produced, Crusoe goes back to his island, now a small, squabbling colony, and tries to set it right by bringing supplies and religion. He also travels widely, to China and through Russia, but the emphasis is on him and his reactions rather than these

strange places themselves. After describing China only to disparage it
as a poor place compared to Europe, Crusoe says that he "shall make
no more descriptions of countries and people; 'tis none of my business,
or any part of my design; but giving an account of my own wandrings,
and a long variety of changes, which perhaps few that come after me
will have heard the like of."[13] The preference is significant. Travel-
adventure narrative such as Defoe wrote treats its exotic locales as arenas
for action, realms to be exploited by the traveler to satisfy his urge for
profitable experience, for self-expression and self-expansion.

Despite his careful piety, Crusoe resembles in his omnivorous desire
for new experiences and in the irrepressible, possessive individuality that
is their result another figure out of the early eighteenth-century popular
imagination, the pirate. Even as he published in 1720 the second sequel
to *Robinson Crusoe, Serious Reflections During the Life and Surprizing
Adventures of Robinson Crusoe: With His Vision of the Angelick World,*
Defoe also published a short life of the notorious pirate, Avery *(The
King of Pirates: Being An Account of the Famous Enterprises of Captain
Avery)* and the long narrative based in part on the careers of real pirates
like Avery, *The Life, Adventures, and Pyracies of the Famous Captain
Singleton.* To be sure, piracy in Defoe's day was as real and pressing
an issue as terrorism is in our own. Warring nations often licensed
shipowners as privateers to attack each other's shipping, but when peace
came some continued to ply the trade, their numbers swelled by out-
of-work sailors. For example, when the War of the Spanish Succession
between England and France ended in 1713 piracy flourished, especially
in Caribbean and North American waters, so that by 1718 as one
historian notes trade in the West Indies was "paralyzed."[14] Defoe's
fascination with pirates goes back at least to 1707, when he devoted
a number of the *Review* to rumors that a group of them, settled in
Madagascar, wished to buy a pardon from the British government with
their fabulous wealth. As concern about piracy mounted, Defoe featured
their activities with other news reports in *Mercurius Politicus: Being
Monthly Observations on the Affairs of Great Britain* during 1718 and
1719. He served (or exploited) continued popular interest with his
comprehensive, two-volume *A General History of the Robberies and
Murders of the most notorious Pyrates, and also Their Policies, Discipline
and Government* (1724).

Although these lives of the pirates, with one interesting exception,
are factual, some of them also evoke the pirate as a compelling figure,
an embodiment of forbidden energies who can be both glamorous and

monstrous. For example, Captain Edward Teach, the notorious "Black-beard," is memorably portrayed, depraved and demonic, his huge beard tied with ribbons, "lighted Matches under his Hat, which appearing on each Side of his Face, his Eyes naturally looking fierce and wild, made him altogether such a Figure, that Imagination cannot Form an Idea of a Fury, from Hell, to look more frightful" (85). So, too, Captain Edward Low, commits bloodcurdling atrocities of which this is typical: when a Portuguese captain jettisons a large sum of money rather than surrender it, Low "rav'd like a Fury, swore a thousand Oaths, and ordered the Captain's Lips to be cut off, which he broil'd before his Face, and afterwards murdered him and all the Crew, being thirty-two Persons" (326). On the other hand, Captain Bartho Roberts fights his last battle gallantly, "dressed in a rich crimson Damask Wastcoat and Breeches, and Feather in his Hat, a Gold Chain round his Neck, with a Diamond Cross hanging to it, a Sword in his Hand, and two Pair of Pistols hanging at the End of a Silk Sling, slung over his Shoulders" (243).

Captain Roberts, before his gallant end, was hugely successful, taking between 1719 and 1722 nearly four hundred ships.[15] Roberts's summary of his motives for turning pirate tells us a good deal about the appeal of such figures. Roberts admits frankly that he has not been forced into crime by circumstances; rather, he has chosen to "get rid of the disagreeable Superiority of some Masters," to forsake the "thin Commons, low Wages, and hard Labour" of honest service for "Plenty and Satiety, Pleasure and Ease, Liberty and Power" (244). Of course, Defoe disowns such rogues as Roberts, explaining that his revolt is a set of "deprav'd Propensities" (84). But like other eighteenth-century writers such as Gay and Fielding, Defoe was attracted to the satiric possibilities of the romantic criminal, who can serve as a revealing exaggeration in his naked, rebellious individualism of the motives underlying ordinary economic behavior. "It would make a sad chasm on the Exchange of London," he remarked in the *Review,* "if all the pirates should be taken away from among the merchants there."[16] Moreover, purged of its self-seeking ferocity, the myth of the pirate and his community of rebels can form a utopian criticism of social injustice and hypocrisy. Some of Defoe's real pirates serve both these purposes; Captain White refuses to rob from women and children, Captain North is just and honest with his victims, and Captain Bellamy vigorously expresses the injustice of the class system. But his clearest exploitation of the satiric possibilities of piracy is the wholly fictional life of Captain Misson, a

French naval officer who turns pirate and flies a white flag with the motto "A Deo a Libertate, For God and Liberty, as an Emblem of our Uprightness and Resolution" (393).[17] Through his lieutenant and advisor, the defrocked priest Caraccioli, Misson rejects the black flag of ordinary pirates: "they were no Pyrates, but Men who were resolved to assert that Liberty which God and Nature gave them, and own no Subjection to any, farther than was for the common Good of all." Presenting a radical version of Defoe's own views on the right to rebel against unjust governments, Caraccioli concludes that "it speaks a generous and great Soul to shake off the Yoak; and if we cannot redress our Wrongs, withdraw from sharing the Miseries which meaner Spirits submit to, and scorn to yield to the Tyranny" (393).

Although much of this is actually for a contemporary English audience an uncontroversial attack on French absolutism, Defoe clearly took pleasure in the subversive implications of radical ideas and "Of Captain Misson" is one of the longest biographies in the two volumes of *A General History of the Pyrates.* How to account, then, for the lack of similar moral and political implications in Defoe's most elaborate fictional treatment of piracy, *Captain Singleton?* What seems clear is that extended fiction demanded more attention to plot, scene, and characterization and less to ideology. Obviously, Defoe realized that his audience wanted the pleasures of action and exotic scene rather than the stimulation of radical ideas.

A travel narrative grafted on to pirate biography, *Captain Singleton* has its origins in Defoe's wide reading in collections of voyages like the Elizabethan Richard Hakluyt's as well as popular contemporary accounts like William Dampier's. Specifically, Defoe found much of his material in Robert Knox's *Historical Relation of Ceylon* (1681), a story of nineteen years in captivity on what is now Sri Lanka. The most memorable part of Defoe's book is a trek clear across Africa, from east to west, then largely unexplored and unknown. Captain Bob, as he calls himself, is also a fabulously successful pirate, but the center of the book insofar as it approaches the novelistic quality of Defoe's other narratives is the personality of its hero. To conventional pirate biography, Defoe added his persistent interest in simulating personal authenticity. Bob Singleton begins life with an innocence or ignorance that is equivalent to Crusoe's physical isolation. Kidnapped as a child of two and sold to a beggar, then to a gypsy, he is a ward of various parishes until adopted by a master of a ship who takes him to sea. Captured by Moorish pirates and then rescued by Portuguese men-of-war, Bob finds himself in Lisbon, alone when his master dies of wounds, unable to speak the language and equally unable to understand anything about his situation. After all the other English sailors have dispersed, Bob simply stays in the ship, "almost reduced to my primitive state, viz. of starving."[18] Told by an old sailor in broken English that he must leave, Bob answers: "Whither must I go (said I?) Where you will, (said he), Home to your own country, if you will. How must I go thither (said I?) Why have you no friend (said he?) No, (said I) not in the world, but that dog, pointing to the ship's dog, (who having stole a piece of meat just before, had brought it close by me, and I had taken it from him, and eat it) for he has been a good friend, and brought me my dinner" (5).

Bob becomes this old sailor's servant and in due course learns enough to get by—some Portuguese and some navigation and especially "to be an errant thief and a bad sailor" (6). But he never becomes quite like his various comrades. Using a fairly crude narrative strategy, Defoe makes Bob innocent rather than wicked so that he can emerge as an instinctively skillful adventurer, a morally neutral blank slate on which experience can write. A sort of working-class Crusoe, Bob drifts into a mutiny without any of the self-consciousness or ideological posturing of the pirate at his most articulate: "I was as ripe for any villainy, as a young fellow that had no solid thought ever placed in his mind could be supposed to be. . . . All the little scenes of life I had pass'd thro', had been full of dangers and desperate circumstances; but I was either so young, or so stupid, that I escaped the grief and anxiety of them, for want of having a sense of their tendency and consequences" (14). In the long run, escaping the consequences of "desperate circumstances" is what makes a hero in Defoe's fiction, which is despite its realism founded on a contradiction. On the one hand, his novels implicitly argue that individuals are produced by determining environments, but on the other hand they dramatize how by skill, patience, and luck (except Defoe chooses to call it Providence) those circumstances can be eluded. In *Captain Singleton* more than in his other books, Defoe seems to be operating on the principle that the ideal hero needs to be less than fully conscious of the impossibility of his job.

Ready for anything that offers, Bob is the morally innocent adventurer, a boy who leads men rather like Robert Louis Stevenson's Jim Hawkins in *Treasure Island*. When his comrades decide to build a large canoe to attempt to escape from Madagascar, Bob's advice that they turn pirates has the wisdom of the serpent and the innocence of the dove:

I conceiv'd our business was not to attempt our escape in a canoe, but that
as there were other vessels at sea besides our ship, and that there were few
nations that lived on the sea-shore that were so barbarous, but that they
went to sea in some boats or other, our business was to cruise along the
coast of the island, which was very long, and to seize upon the first we
could get that was better than our own, and so from that to another, till
perhaps we might at last get a good ship to carry us whither ever we pleased
to go. (30)

As his mates hesitate fearfully, Bob urges action, earning their grudging
respect: "Well done, pyrate, said the gunner, he that had look'd in
my hand, and told me I should come to the gallows; I'll say that for
him, says he, he always looks the same way. But I think o' my
conscience, 'tis our only way now. Don't tell me, says I, of being a
pyrate, we must be pyrates, or any thing, to get fairly out of this
cursed place" (36).

   In what follows, Bob's gaze is steadily outward, avoiding introspection
and irresolution, never flinching in the face of sensationally appalling
prospects. "We were now landed upon the continent of Africa, the
most desolate, desart, and unhospitable country in the world, even
Greenland and Nova Zembla it self not excepted" (58). Repeatedly,
Bob invokes that prospect as they struggle across the immense continent:
"a vast howling wilderness, not a tree, a river, or a green thing to be
seen, for as far as the eye could look; nothing but a scalding sand,
which as the wind blew, drove about in clouds, enough to overwhelm
man and beast" (96–97). Now surrounded at night by roaring animals,
"innumerable numbers of devilish creatures" (123), then arriving again
at the bleakest of vistas ("as far as the eye could look, south, or west,
or north-west, there was nothing to be seen but a vast howling wilderness,
with neither tree or river, or any green thing" [137]); Bob and his
men exemplify the resourcefulness that is the signature of Defoe's heroes.
Like Crusoe, they treat the natives as handy raw materials, using them
where possible as slaves, mowing them down in great numbers with
shot and shell when they resist or prove hostile, and trading with them
for food. A key figure in all this, a more immediately skillful Crusoe,
is "the Cutler," who makes objects out of metal to trade with the
natives, wild fire at night to keep away predatory animals, and constructs
a scale when they discover gold to divide it equally among them. The
rigors of the journey are, in fact, rewarded by this gold at its end. The
scene is a carefree fantasy in which priceless raw materials are obtained

by European skill and imagination, the terrifying fauna of the continent tamed and parodied in the images the cutler fashions: "All the while we were busy washing gold dust out of the rivers, and our negroes the like, our ingenious cutler was hammering and cutting, and he was grown so dexterous by use, that he formed all manner of images. He cut out elephants, tygers, civet cats, ostriches, eagles, cranes, fowls, fishes, and indeed whatever he pleased, in thin plates of hammer'd gold, for his silver and iron was almost all gone" (159).

But spectacle and ingenuity aside, there is little in *Captain Singleton* to hold the reader. When the African adventure is over, Bob gets to London, spends his money, and goes back to sea, turning pirate in due course. Defoe deliberately avoids moral and psychological issues and has Bob summarize this crucial transition very quickly. "I even rage in my own thoughts to reflect upon the manner how it [his money] was wasted, so I need record no more; the rest merits to be conceal'd with blushes, for that it was spent in all kinds of folly and wickedness" (168). The rest is a series of piratical encounters as sweeping as the trek across Africa—from the Canary Islands to the West Indies to Madagascar to the Indian Ocean to the Philippines to Formosa— modeled on the biography of Captain Avery that Defoe had published that same year.

Captain Singleton anticipates Defoe's achievements in his subsequent narratives by lightly sketching in their characteristic patterns of relationships. Following the dictates of popular taste for criminal lives, Defoe manifests his own fascination with survival at the margins of society. He inserts into the mindless episodic sensationalism he thought his public would buy two themes that recur in his fiction: first, an intensely coherent observation of specific techniques of survival and domination that gives them archetypal resonances similar to those in *Robinson Crusoe;* second, a satirical humor and moral casuistry whereby the conventional individuals of criminal biography display flashes of intelligence and personality.

In *Captain Singleton,* these latter are provided mainly by the Quaker William Walters, a surgeon Bob's crew captures in one of their forays. William agrees to go along with the pirates but demands written certification "that I was taken away by force, and against my will," promising to make himself useful but preserving his technical innocence: "thou knowest it is not my business to meddle when thou art to fight" (175). In time, William becomes virtual leader of the pirates, moderating their savagery by his cunning. As Manuel Schonhorn suggests, he brings "comic relief to a situation rife with expected violence and potential brutalities." William enables Defoe to turn his narrative away from the reckless immorality of actual piracy and toward enlightened moral and economic self-interest. To some extent, Defoe through William undermines pirate biography; in Schonhorn's words, he "dilutes beyond distinction what is falsely represented as a traditional buccaneering narrative filled with daring adventures and piracies."[19] Within the pirate community, in historical fact a close-knit small society bound by ties of guilt and mutual protection, William and Bob form a subversive cell, individuals out for themselves. Eventually (when they have grown fabulously rich) William proposes repentance to Bob and arranges their return in disguise to England. When Bob grows suddenly remorseful and wonders how they can truly repent without making restitution, William's answer is shrewdly pragmatic. "We ought to keep it carefully together, with a resolution to do what right with it we are able; and who knows what opportunity Providence may put into our hands to do justice at least to some of those we have injured, so we ought at least to leave it to him, and go on, as it is, without doubt, our present business to do, to some place of safety, where we may wait his will" (322). William converts the adventurer's simple assertiveness into self-reserved intelligence and observant opportunism; he turns Bob's episodic narrative into a purposeful and repentant return home. He preserves the innocent mask of a Quaker amid the brutal honesty of piracy, and in the end saves Bob by arranging their audacious disguise as "Persian" merchants (as Bob notes admiringly "we could not understand or speak one word of the language of Persia, or indeed of any other but English and Dutch" [320]). Although William is only sketchily rendered (Defoe seems more amused with him than any of his other characters), his presence in *Captain Singleton* indicates Defoe's impatience with simple adventure and criminal biography. The narratives he published during the next three years, 1722–24, are all in various ways attempts to complicate popular narrative formats.

Chapter Five
Crime, Adventure, and Domesticity: *Colonel Jack* and *Moll Flanders*

Colonel Jack

As a theme for serious fiction, piracy faded quickly, preserved during the nineteenth century in the popular imagination of the English-speaking world in children's stories and comic opera and in our own time in swashbuckling films of adventure on the Spanish Main. As a basis for adventure narrative, piracy may have proved too melodramatic an occupation for Defoe to handle, perhaps too improbable and romantic or too brutal a set of circumstances from which to extract the kind of adventure he (or his audience) preferred. *Captain Singleton* attempts to move away from the pattern of *Robinson Crusoe,* in which as Paul Zweig remarks the ethos of adventure is undermined by a story "in which the exotic episodes are flattened relentlessly into the ordinary by the ordinary character of the protagonist."[1] Captain Bob is something like the adventurer Zweig traces in European literature from Odysseus onward, reckless, eager for variety, excitement, and the thrilling uncertainty of what must be (if it is to be truly adventurous) an essentially episodic life, free of the stability of marriage and family. But Defoe also turns Bob toward a perfunctory sort of repentance, arranging a return home and marriage (to William's sister) that rejects the episodic excitement of the adventure story. *Captain Singleton* thus has a small measure of autobiographical complexity, as Bob comes to something like moral self-consciousness and is integrated into society at last.

The History and Remarkable Life of the Truly Honourable Col. Jacque, Commonly Call'd Col. Jack (1722) also complicates some simple literary patterns; it is a virtual anthology of marketable themes such as Defoe treated more single-mindedly in other works during these years. *Colonel Jack* begins as criminal autobiography, then turns to pseudohistorical memoir, and includes a good deal of domestic and marital incident, resembling as it proceeds books like *Moll Flanders* (1722), *Memoirs of a Cavalier* (1720), and *Roxana* (1724). At first glance, the opening sequences of *Colonel Jack* look like a replay of *Captain Singleton,* as Defoe traces Jack's career as a street urchin and pickpocket in the streets of London. Jack is no ordinary street boy. Defoe gives him moral sensitivity and fills him with aspirations to become a "gentleman" that set him distinctly apart from his companions. Bob Singleton is likewise set apart by circumstances, an English orphan boy among Portuguese seamen, forced to learn to survive by his wits somewhat like the heroes of the Spanish picaresque tradition, out like them to trick a cruel and unjust world, a precociously clever rogue in a world of rogues.[2] But, even as he picks pockets and commits highway robbery, Colonel Jack is never simply a rogue from a literary tradition; he is more like a real victim of urban circumstances, a young criminal of course but also in Defoe's rendering both the result of and the moral exception to the proletarian brutality all around him.

Defoe was as usual both responding to his audience's demands and modifying a popular tradition. From at least the Restoration, criminal narratives were widely read in England, encompassing a variety of forms: reports of crimes committed, notorious criminals captured and sometimes escaping, summaries of trials and transcripts of dying speeches, descriptions from prison cell and gallows of the psychological and spiritual condition of the condemned, and sometimes fairly extensive biographies of prominent villains. There seems to have been a surge in crime in England from 1715 to 1725, and Defoe as Maximillian E. Novak observes became "the mythologist of this crime wave."[3] Between 1720 and 1726 Defoe wrote for the Tory periodical *Applebee's Original Weekly Journal,* which featured criminal lives. As "Mr. Applebee's Man" Defoe interviewed famous criminals in their cells or at the scaffold and claimed to have received the manuscripts of their lives (which he had of course previously composed).[4] And he published a number of pamphlet biographies of notorious criminals, notably two each of Jack Sheppard and Jonathan Wild.

In many ways, the early pages of *Colonel Jack* are the most interesting, original part of the book, an occasionally vivid rendering of a juvenile underworld. These pages derive from the criminal journalism Defoe himself practiced, but they very quickly demonstrate his distaste for the myth of the criminal as folk hero that it tended to promote. Jack is a nameless bastard who finds himself at ten years old on his own in the streets, part of a gang of homeless children.[5] His description of himself invokes the teeming streets of London at their most unlovely. "As for my person, while I was a dirty glass-bottle house boy, sleeping in the ashes, and dealing always in the street dirt, it cannot be expected but that I look'd like what I was, and so we did all; that is to say, like a *black your shoes your honour,* a beggar boy, a black-guard boy, or what you please, despicable, and miserable, to the last degree" (7).

Gangs of homeless children like Jack were a growing source of concern for many in the early decades of the century. With many other social commentators of the day, Defoe thought that "Charity Schools," where poor boys and girls were taught to read the Bible, were a sensible response to the problem. One opponent of charity schools, Bernard Mandeville, describes in 1723 the urban scene quite as vividly as Defoe: "in every open place [you] meet with a Company of Black-guards without Shirts or any thing whole about them, that insensible of their Misery are continually increasing it with Oaths and Imprecations! Can anyone doubt but these are the great Nursery of Thieves and Pick-pockets?"[6] Jack's rendition of his life as a child fits Mandeville's evocation and may just shock a reader who assumes that modern cities are uniquely cruel and indifferent:

Thus we all made a shift, tho' we were so little, to keep from starving, [by begging and running errands] and as for lodging, we lay in the summer-time about the watch-houses, and on bulk-heads, and shop-doors, where we were known; as for a bed we knew nothing what belong'd to it for many years after my nurse died, and in winter we got into the ash-holes, and nealing arches [under which hot glass was set to cool] in the glass-house, call'd Dallows's glass-house, near Rosemary-Lane, or at another glass-house in Ratcliff-high-way. In this manner we liv'd for some years, and here we fail'd not to fall among a gang of naked, ragged rogues like ourselves, wicked as the devil cou'd desire to have them be, at so early an age, and ripe for all the other parts of mischief that suited them as they advanc'd in years. (9)

Again, Mandeville can attest to the plausibility of Jack's childhood as one of a gang of pick-pockets. "In a populous City," he writes, "it is not difficult for a young Rascal, that has pushed himself into a Crowd, with a small Hand and nimble Fingers to whip away a Handkerchief or Snuff-Box from a Man who is thinking on Business, and regardless of his Pocket." "Over-grown Cities," like Paris and London, "harbour Rogues and Villains as Granaries do Vermin; they

afford a perpetual Shelter to the worst of People, and are places of
Safety to Thousands of Criminals."[7] In Mandeville's arresting image of
vermin in a granary, London is a menacing labyrinth of competing
small predators. Defoe resists such melodrama by making Jack a pathetic
street boy. For example, Jack returns for a reward a merchant's financial
document wallet (stolen by his instructor in crime, an older boy named
Will). The merchant and his friend engage Jack in a movingly simple
dialogue that qualifies Jack's happy-go-lucky summary of his boyish
days.

Well, says he, What wil't thou do with this money now thou hast it? I
don't know, said I. Where will you put it? said he. In my pocket, said I.
In your pocket, said he, is your pocket whole? shan't you lose it? Yes, said
I, my pocket is whole. And where will you put it, when you come home?
I have no home, said I, and cry'd again. Poor child! said he then, What
doest thou do for thy Living? I go of errands, said I, for the folks in
Rosemary-lane. And what dost thou do for lodging at night? I lye at the
glass-house, said I, at night. How lye at the glass-house! have they any beds
there? says he. I never lay in a bed in my life, said I, as I remember. Why?
says he, what do you lye on at the glass-house? The ground, says I, and
sometimes a little straw, or upon the warm ashes. Here the gentleman, that
lost the bills, said, this poor child is enough to make a man weep for the
miseries of humane nature, and be thankful for himself, he puts tears into
my eyes; and into mine too, says the other. (37)

   Two complementary attitudes thus run through the book's early
pages: moral outrage over urban squalor and the crime it breeds is
what a modern reader may feel and is probably part of Defoe's attitude,
but Jack's narrative of his childhood emphasizes its pathos. Like the
shocked merchants, Defoe's audience is meant to weep at the picture
of urban waifs, deprived of even the simplest necessities, innocently
enjoying the proceeds of petty thievery. With "Major Jack," his younger
chum, Jack first splurges on warm stockings and dry shoes, "things, I
say, which I had not been acquainted with a great while" (15), and
then on their first decent meal: "so we went to a boiling cook's in
Rosemary-Lane, where we treated our selves nobly, and as I thought
with my self we began to live like Gentlemen, for we had three-penny-
worth of boil'd beef, two-penny-worth of pudding, a penny brick, (as
they call it, or loaf) and a whole pint of strong beer, which was seven
pence in all" (15).

Next to this sweetly sentimental picture of a juvenile underclass, Defoe has Jack deliver its encircling brutalities of crime and punishment. "Captain Jack," his older and bolder friend, is whipped for taking part in a kidnapping, and Jack is "frighted almost to death" as he watches. "I saw him afterwards, with his back all wheal'd with the lashes, and in several places bloody, and thought I should have died with the sight of it; but I grew better acquainted with those things afterwards" (13). Unlike his friends, however, Jack never loses his fear, and his adolescence is darkened by the lengthening shadow of the gallows. At eighteen, Jack runs with a marauding gang of youths, roaming the outer edges of London and brutally robbing whoever comes along. But shortly afterwards, the gangleader, Will, is arrested and taken to Newgate: "my very joints trembl'd, and I was ready to sink into the ground, and all that evening, and that night following, I was in the uttermost consternation; my head run upon nothing but *Newgate,* and the gallows, and being hang'd" (75).

Colonel Jack begins as a realistic glimpse for comfortably situated readers of a criminal milieu. But if Jack is to hold the reader's interest he must, somewhat mysteriously and improbably, acquire a distinctive identity and become more than just another member of the criminal class. Even as Defoe works to render that world of urban criminality, he must also work at canceling part of its reality as compelling social circumstances. Defoe has to make his audience aware that Jack is of interest precisely as a rare exception who eludes the consequences of that environment but has no illusions about the difficulties of beating the odds: " 'tis very seldom that the unfortunate are so but for a day, as the great rise by degrees of greatness to the pitch of glory, in which they shine, so the miserable sink to the depth of their misery by a continu'd series of disaster, and are long in the tortures and agonies of their distress'd circumstances before a turn of fortune, if ever such a thing happens to them, give them a prospect of deliverance" (4).

But more than "a turn of fortune" is responsible for Jack's deliverance. Morally and intellectually, Jack insists from the opening pages, he stood apart from his miserable companions. As Jack describes himself, the child is father to the man, precociously verbal and intellectually curious. "Always upon the inquiry, asking questions of things done in publick as well as in private," Jack calls himself "a kind of an historian," constructing from what he hears "a tollerable account of what had been done, and of what was then a doing in the world"(10–11). Jack takes special pleasure in remembering how his verbal talents make him appear to be what he is not (a recurring moment in Defoe's fiction). "I remember very well," he says at the very beginning of the story, "that when I was carried before a justice for a theft which indeed I was not guilty of, and defended my self by argument . . . the justice told me it was pitty I had not been better employ'd, for I was certainly better taught." The justice is mistaken, but Jack explains that he "had a natural talent of talking, and could say as much to the purpose as most people that had been taught no more than I" (7).

The only explanation Jack offers for his distinctiveness is his lifelong obsession with "gentility." Told by the woman who brings him up that his father was "a man of quality" and his mother a "gentlewoman," little Jack is made self-conscious of his difference, his father having instructed the woman "to bid me *remember, that I was a gentleman,* and this he said was all the education he would desire of her for me, for he did not doubt, he said, but that sometime or other the very hint would inspire me with thoughts suitable to my birth, and that I would certainly act like a gentleman, if I believed myself to be so" (3). And yet, except for that hint, he is brought up just like the two other "sons of shame" his nurse takes on. They turn out to be incorrigible characters who come to predictably bad ends, one hanged as a high-wayman, the other "broke upon the wheel" in Paris (185). From the first, Jack is full of guilt, "a strange kind of uninstructed conscience" that makes him an uneasy pickpocket, "tormented about it, that I could not rest night or day, while I made the people easie, from whom the things were taken" (55). "Something in me," Jack muses, "by what secret influence I knew not, kept me from the other degrees of raking and vice, and in short, from the general wickedness of the rest of my companions" (60).

Defoe himself clearly believed that real gentlemen are made rather than born. He thought of himself as having achieved middle-class status by education and hard work. As he wrote in *The Compleat English Gentleman* at the very end of his life, authentic gentility involves more than money and privilege: "when learning, education, virtue and good manners are wanting or degenerated and corrupted in a gentleman, he sinks out of the rank, ceases to be any more a gentleman, and is, *ipso facto,* turn'd back among the less despicable Throng of the *Plebeii.*"[8] So Jack's pathetic fantasy that he is bound to be a gentleman has little to do with the realities of social status as Defoe understood them. But in imagining young Jack Defoe shows how powerful a motive the illusion of social difference can be, and whatever moral irony he may have intended to create is dissipated by the ultimate effectiveness of Jack's desire. Jack's conviction of his uniqueness does in fact form him as an individual; his identity depends precisely on his resistance to the norms of his group, and the validity of his sense of gentility is therefore not an issue. What matters is that such feelings provide Jack with a sense of self and with a motive for self-improvement. As David Blewett remarks, *Colonel Jack* is unified to some extent by its "preoccupation with the ambiguities of identity and disguise, reality and illusion, and with the irony that gentility itself may be a mode of deception."⁹ *Colonel Jack* is a realistic study of personality to the extent that it dramatizes how individuality is a created identity rather than an essence, a series of masks and roles founded in this case on Jack's half-baked notion of his gentility.

To achieve characterization as well as action, Defoe needed to emphasize Jack's vague sense of destiny in order to overcome the merely episodic tendency of this sort of fiction. Like his other narratives, *Colonel Jack* boasts on its title page of the amazing variety of scene and incident it contains. Jack was "born a gentleman, put 'prentice to a pick-pocket, was six and twenty years a thief, and then kidnapp'd to Virginia. Came back a merchant, married four wives, . . . went into the wars, behav'd bravely, got preferment, was made Colonel of a regiment, came over, and fled with the Chevalier, and is now abroad compleating a life of wonders." All those separate incidents have their own particular vividness, and Defoe seems to take particular pleasure in the varied specifics of Jack's movements through these widely scattered scenes. But to some extent Jack's self-consciousness holds that variety together. More than just a collection of incidents in unusual places, the narrative carefully records crucial phases in Jack's development from innocence to mature and complex identity.

For example, Jack and his friend Captain Jack run away from London and end up in Edinburgh. As they arrive, they are shocked by the sight of two men, who turn out to be pickpockets, being whipped through the streets, held on a long leash. The scene is carefully arranged so that the two Jacks see the men, naked to the waist, running what appears at first to be "a race for some mighty wager" (100). The truth is revealed when the runners are pulled up short by the lines that hold them and a man appears who gives "each of them two frightful lashes with a wire-whipe." This man, Jack explains, "was the city hangman; who (by the way) is there an officer of note, has a constant sallary, and is a man of substance, and not only so, but a most dextrous fellow

in his office; and makes a great deal of money of his employment"
(100–101). Jack balances fear with appreciation of the fitness of
institutionalized punishment and admiration for its official administrator.
In part, the scene is a colorful report on this odd Scottish penal custom,
but it is also a contribution to Jack's inner life, another terrible scene
of punishment to drive him on. As he says a bit later when he enlists
in the army, "I had a secret satisfaction at being now under no necessity
of stealing, and living in fear of a prison, and of the lash of the
hangman; a thing which from the time I saw it in Edinborough, was
so terrible to me, that I could not think of it without horror" (104).

Jack's admiration for the hangman in Edinburgh anticipates his own
transformation, after he is shanghaied to Virginia, from indentured
servant to overseer who develops a mode of punishment for his master's
slaves whereby the simple brutality with which they are treated is
replaced by psychological manipulation that wins their devotion. Because
he is tenderhearted and reluctant to practice the customary cruelty, Jack
threatens the slaves with punishments but then tells them they have
been saved by the mercy of the "Great Master" who owns the plantations.
Jack claims that he thus effects a reform whose results can still be seen:
"they are to this day less cruel and barbarous to their negroes, than
they are in Barbados, and Jamaica; and 'tis observ'd the negroes are
not in these colonies so desperate, neither do they so often run away,
or so often plot mischief against their master, as they do in those"
(149). The Virginia episode thus represents a stage in Jack's development
whereby his accumulated inner life not only defines him as separate
and unique but provides him with an instinctive grasp of the psychology
of punishment and discipline. What Jack has internalized enables him
to transform the outer world to his own advantage and in his own
image.

Defoe was an enthusiastic promoter of English colonial expansion,
and Colonel Jack presents himself as a shining example of how "the
most despicable ruin'd man in the world, has here a fair opportunity
put into his hands to begin the world again" (153). But mere economic
rehabilitation is never quite enough for Defoe's characters. On one level,
Defoe was more interested in spiritual development, and even as they
prosper his autobiographers often struggle to understand God's plan in
what appear to be the random events of their lives. In Virginia, Jack
seems to come close to that sort of spiritual insight under the guidance
of one of his indentured servants who tutors him in Latin, history, and
eventually in religion. But Jack finds history more engaging than religion.

His uneasiness about his past life wears off "gradually, as such things generally do, where the first impressions are not deep enough" (171). Instead, Jack forms a "secret resolution, to see more of the world, if possible, and realize those things to my mind, which I had hitherto only entertain'd remote ideas of, by the help of books" (172).

In a simple sense, this development is inevitable. It is too early in the book for Jack to repent or to learn the vanity of earthly striving, and his restlessness in Virginia is a convenient reason to keep the narrative moving. In spite of his interest in the pattern of spiritual autobiography, Defoe communicates through Jack something of his own involvement in contemporary history. In Virginia, Jack may be morally rehabilitated, but he is "as one buried alive, in a remote part of the world" (172). Jack shuns the provincialism, in effect, that Defoe lectured his audience about in the early years of the *Review,* as he warned them against the complacent insularity that failed to understand Louis XIV's ambitions for world dominance. Of course, despite his eager reading of history, both ancient and modern, Jack claims no particular political allegiance; he simply longs to be at the center of things, "in the great war wherein the French king might be said to be engag'd with, and against all the powers of Europe" (172).

Defoe provides a participant's view of some of the most important events in recent European history, placing Jack's brief career as a soldier at the beginning of what was to become the War of the Spanish Succession, which involved England and her allies against France in a struggle for European dominance. From the point of view of most English people in 1722, Jack's service with an Irish regiment in the French army fighting the Austrians in Italy in 1701–2 and his subsequent commission as an officer with troops attached to the Old Pretender in an abortive French invasion of England are grossly treasonous. But that treason seems to be part of the complicated difficulties that Defoe likes to wrap around his characters. In spite of his naive involvements in crime, war, love, and especially politics, Jack somehow survives, develops new skills, and even prospers, maintaining his special sort of irrepressible individuality. As Defoe inserts Jack in the heart of recent history, he also goes out of his way to preserve his subversive marginality. Jack insists he is neutral, a fascinated spectator at these events rather than a committed participant, out for excitement and military glory exclusively. So when he behaves gallantly with the Irish regiments in the defense of Cremona, and when he is later wounded and taken prisoner, these achievements are primarily for Jack part of a process of self-discovery and expansion: "I now had the satisfaction of knowing, and that for the first time too, that I was not that cowardly low spirited wretch that I was . . . but men never know themselves till they are tried, and courage is acquir'd by time, and experience of things" (208).

Defoe's disappearance behind his fictional autobiographers has made some readers wonder just where he stands and what he wants his readers to think. As Jack wanders into treason and blunders through a series of disastrous marriages, he is clearly the object of some scorn or amusement. Jack himself looks ruefully back on the foolish social climbing that leads to his first marriage: "She came to the house where I lodg'd, as usual, and we were often together, supp'd together, play'd at cards together, danc'd together; for in France I accomplish'd myself with every thing that was needful, to make me what I believ'd myself to be even from a boy, I mean a gentleman" (191). But such accomplishments only lead to betrayal and almost fatal violence. His wife nearly bankrupts him and her lover has Jack assaulted after he refuses to fight a duel with him. Even then, Jack hardly learns his lesson. While a prisoner of war in Italy, he is tricked into marrying and soon finds himself cuckolded once again. His reaction is a sort of comic version of his earlier guilty obsession: "It vext me also to think that it should be my fate to be a cuckold, both abroad and at home, and sometimes I would be in such a rage about it, that I had no government of myself, when I thought of it; whole days, and I may say sometimes whole nights I spent musing and considering what I should do to her" (225). The episode ends seriously, however, as Jack wounds his wife's lover in a duel and has to flee to England.

And yet for all Jack's awkwardness as a husband and in spite of his thoughtless treason as a Jacobite soldier (indeed because of these faults), his original talent for survival and disguise expands and acquires new sophistication. Whatever the supervising moral principles at work in the book as a whole, the narrative communicates pleasure in Jack's resourcefulness as he rebounds from disaster and escapes the full consequences of his foolish actions. The last third or so of the book shifts the narrative emphasis, in fact, from Jack's inner development and his fits of incomplete self-awareness to his successful evasions and inventions. Jack becomes most himself by relinquishing the idea of a single self, finding his most comfortable identity in assuming multiple identities. For example, here he is in England after his second marriage, a fugitive from French justice and of course a traitor in the eyes of English law:

I was now in my native country, where my circumstances were easy; and tho' I had had ill luck abroad, for I brought little home with me; yet by [a] little good mannagement, I might soon have money by me. I had no body to keep but my self, and my plantations in Virginia, generally return'd me from 400 to 600£. a year, one year above 700£. and to go thither, I concluded, was to be bury'd a-live; so I put off all thoughts of it, and resolv'd to settle somewhere in England, where I might know every body, and no body know me. I was not long in concluding where to pitch, for as I spoke the French tongue perfectly well, having been so many years among them, it was easy for me to pass for a French man. So I went to Canterbury, call'd my self an English Man, among the French; and a French man among the English; and on that score, was the more perfectly concealed, going by the name of Monsieur Charnot, with the French, was call'd Mr. Charnock among the English. Here, indeed, I liv'd perfectly *Incog.* I made no particular acquaintance, so as to be intimate, and yet I knew every body, and every body knew me; I discours'd in common, talk'd French with the Walloons; and English, with the English; and living retir'd and sober, was well enough receiv'd by all sorts; but as I medled with no bodies business, so no body meddl'd with mine; I thought I liv'd pretty well. (233–34)

Like Defoe himself spying in Scotland for Harley twenty years earlier, Jack in Canterbury is all things to all men.[10] His sometimes humiliating experience in the world, on the great stage of history and in the lesser arena of domestic and social strife, now enables him to manipulate the world and to avoid the consequences of his actions. Whatever the self-conscious moral purpose of his narratives, Defoe reveals in the precise intricacies of passages like these a fascinated admiration for amoral individualism, that is, for brilliantly improvised strategies whereby his characters can, for a time anyway, exercise control over others, becoming themselves by withholding themselves. The world—the thickly truthful historical and social setting Defoe often delivers—tends to become merely a challenging arena for private survival and illegal prosperity, evoked just so that it can be manipulated.

Defoe insures, in one respect, that we never lose sight of Jack's awkwardness and the mistakes that require him to construct these elaborate schemes for living. To some extent, his cool seclusion breaks down, and he becomes disastrously involved in the Jacobite uprising of 1715. Safe as he thinks once again in Virginia, his past comes back one day to haunt him in the shape of transported fellow rebels. But his past also saves him, for he has discovered among his indentured servants his faithless first wife, now repentant and still desirable, made wise by misfortunes. In a sequence too complicated for exact summary, she talks him out of his panic and devises a plan of escape. While she goes to London to see about a pardon, Jack embarks on the first of what is eventually a series of fabulously successful smuggling voyages into the Spanish Caribbean.

From the point of view of narrative economy and coherence, these voyages are unnecessary, a repetition of Jack's earlier escapes from the consequences of his past. And yet Defoe takes special care to explain in some detail just how Jack gets around the ban on non-Spanish imports into Cuba and Mexico. Jack's narrative virtually turns into a bill of lading and a ledger, as cargoes are itemized and profits added up: "The chief of the cargo we bought here was fine English broad cloth, serges, drugets, Norwich stuffs, bays, says, and all kinds of woollen manufactures, as also linnen of all sorts, a very great quantity, and near a thousand pounds in fine silks of several sorts. . . . I clear'd in these three months five and twenty thousand pounds sterling in ready money" (293, 296). Defoe seems to take particular delight in showing how Jack transforms his initial capture by the Spaniards off Cuba into large profits. And at the very end, on his last trading voyage, when Jack is forced to take refuge in Mexico with his contraband, Defoe sees to it that he leads a life of splendid comfort, protected by his Spanish merchant friends and realizing a profit of "8570 pieces of eight . . . so that I was indeed, still very rich, all things consider'd" (303).

Here in this elegant retreat Jack begins to repent and to compose the memoirs we have been reading. Now he sees "clearer than ever I had done before, how an invisible over-ruling power, a hand influenced from above, governs all our actions of every kind, limits all our designs, and orders the events of every thing relating to us" (308). Every one of Defoe's fictional autobiographers claims to learn this lesson. In Jack's case, it seems obviously false, far too neat, much too late to change our view of Jack as a resourceful if often somewhat clumsy manager of his fate. For many modern readers of Defoe what does ring true is the inconsistent and thereby authentic personality of the storyteller, whose confusion about the causes of behavior is part of the truth the narrative delivers. As Everett Zimmerman perceptively remarks, all Defoe's characters are "created by a mass of external information, but their internal principles of coherence remain obscure. They impose varying patterns of explanation upon their lives in order to supply coherence and integrity where none is apparent."[11] Jack's deluded search for gentility is one such pattern, and in fact his perfunctory conversion at the end is just another, less convincing attempt to supply coherence. It can be argued that such incoherence is one result of Defoe's hasty, improvisational writing, inevitable for a hard-pressed journalist, churning out books and essays at phenomenal speed.

Moll Flanders

Critics have always recognized that Defoe's strong suit is the richly particularized incident, his weakness developing connections between episodes. At first glance, *Moll Flanders* (1722) looks like the most formlessly episodic of Defoe's books, with over a hundred separate scenes tied together by rapid synopses of other events.[12] And yet most critics would agree that Moll is Defoe's most memorable character, her story the most widely read and highly regarded of Defoe's fictions in the last fifty years. Where Jack seems a shadowy figure, an excuse for stringing adventures together, Moll has struck many readers as profoundly real. Her concreteness may be partially the result of her narrative's narrower setting; she spends most of her time in and around London. But a more important reason for the relative depth and unity of characterization Defoe achieves lies in her gender. As a woman of no fixed social position and limited financial possibilities, she has a unifying and recurring problem: female survival in a masculine world. But richly varied as they are, the episodes in *Moll Flanders* are not a plot in any strict sense; they do not all fit together like a jigsaw puzzle, and one could safely omit some or rearrange others. Taken as a whole, however, they do have a degree of continuity, evoking much more convincingly than *Colonel Jack* a dense tangle of sexual, economic, and moral relationships between self and society.

Like all Defoe's books, *Moll Flanders* has its origin in a popular genre. A criminal biography, based loosely on the lives of two famous thieves, Moll King and Callico Sarah,[13] the book pretends to be a documentary, like *Colonel Jack,* crowded with a variety of incidents in actual places: *The Fortunes and Misfortunes of the Famous Moll Flanders, who was born in Newgate, and during a life of continu'd variety for threescore years, besides her childhood, was twelve year a whore, five times a wife (whereof once to her own brother) twelve year a thief, eight year a transported felon in Virginia, at last grew rich, liv'd honest, and died a penitent, written from her own memorandums.* Although it is far more detailed and complicated than they are, *Moll Flanders* has important affinities with the criminal narratives it imitates. Much of the moral ambiguity in *Moll Flanders* derives from its origins in criminal biography, for as a literary and moral type, the criminal in the early eighteenth century (and now, perhaps) excites a mixture of moral disgust and fascination. Thus, Defoe's characterization of the infamous Jonathan Wild in his 1725 biography stresses Wild's singular, even unique courage: "It must be allowed to Jonathan's fame, that as he steered among rocks and dangerous shoals, so he was a bold pilot; he ventured in and always got out in a manner equally superior; no man ever did the like before him, and I say no man will attempt to do the like after him."[14] To write about a criminal, of course, requires some justification; the subject has to deserve the limelight by being a monster of vice (like Jonathan Wild) or sometimes by being the best at the trade, never just a run-of-the-mill criminal. For example, Moll is hardly modest about her accomplishments as a thief. "I grew the greatest artist of my time, and work'd myself out of every danger," she brags, and goes on to note that where other thieves were in Newgate prison after six months, she worked for more than five years "and the people at Newgate, did not so much as know me; they had heard much of me indeed, and often expected me there; but I always got off, tho' many times in the extreamest danger."[15] Even as Moll records with shame her "hardening" in crime, she still reports her unparalleled success at it, celebrating her fame even as she deplores its cause: "I grew more harden'd and audacious than ever, and the success I had, made my name as famous as any thief of my sort ever had been at Newgate, and in the Old-Bayly" (262).

This blend of repentance and celebration is entirely typical of criminal biography, and it can be seen in cruder fashion in Defoe's own criminal biographies. For example, *The History of the remarkable Life of John Sheppard* (1724) validates as fact the incredible events of Sheppard's career as housebreaker and escape artist: "His history will astonish! and is not compos'd of fiction, fable, or stories plac'd at York, Rome, or Jamaica, but facts done at your doors, facts unheard of, altogether new, incredible, and yet uncontestable."[16] In due course, Defoe's narrator is implicitly contemptuous of Sheppard's vulgar fame: "His escape and his being so suddenly re-taken made such a noise in the town, that it was thought all the common people would have gone mad about him; there being not a porter to be had for love nor money, nor getting into an ale-house, for butchers, shoemakers and barbers, all engag'd in controversies, and wagers, about Sheppard" (186). But the overall effect is mitigation of Sheppard's guilt by detailed, admiring examination of his criminal techniques. The officers at Newgate, the narrator concludes, are not to blame for Sheppard's escapes. "They are but men, and have had to deal with a creature something more than man, a Proteus, supernatural. Words cannot describe him, his actions and workmanship which are too visible, best testifie him" (200). But Defoe describes that workmanship at some length, dwelling with evident satisfaction on the smallest particulars. Visiting the scene of the escape, the narrator reports: "Three screws are visibly taken off the lock, and the doors as strong as art could make them, forc'd open: The locks and bolts either wrench'd or broke, and the cases and other irons made for their security cut asunder: An iron spike broke off from the hatch in the chapel, which he fix'd in the wall and fasten'd his blanket to it, to drop on the leads of Mr. Bird's house; his stockings were found on the leads of Newgate; 'tis question'd whether sixty pounds will repair the damage done to the jayl" (198).

In all his work, fiction and factual journalism, Defoe is powerfully drawn to precisely how trades and crafts operate. This elaboration of techniques has a momentum of its own that blurs moral considerations, and crime becomes in the telling another set of fascinating procedures perfectly executed by masters like Sheppard or, in another, less violent mode, like Moll Flanders. Moll's skills as a thief are more subtle than Sheppard's spectacular escapes, a matter of watching for opportunity, walking the city and taking advantage of the rich prizes there, mastering the arts of disguise and social impersonation. This is how a confederate teaches Moll the art of stealing gold watches from ladies:

At length she put me to practise, she had shewn me her art, and I had several times unhook'd a watch from her own side with great dexterity; at last she show'd me a prize, and this was a young lady big with child who had a charming watch, the thing was to be done as she came out of church; she goes on one side of the lady, and pretends, just as she came to the steps, to fall, and fell against the lady with so much violence as put her into a great fright, and both cry'd out terribly; in the very moment that she jostl'd the lady, I had hold of the watch, and holding it the right way, the start she gave drew the hook out and she never felt it; I made off immediately, and left my schoolmistress to come out of her pretended fright gradually, and the lady too; and presently the watch was miss'd; ay, says my comrade, then it was those rogues that thrust me down, I warrant ye; I wonder the gentlewoman did not miss her watch before, then we might have taken them. (201–2)

And yet the difference between the sketchy sensationalism of criminal biography and the novelistic fullness of *Moll Flanders* is also apparent. Even as Moll describes with obvious satisfaction how she mastered her trade, she also dwells on the moral and psychological significance of that satisfaction. Moll realizes, as she looks back, that this marks a new phase in her career. Drawn into crime by poverty, Moll continues in it even though she might well live honestly if poorly by her needle. "But practise had hardened me, and I grew audacious to the last degree; and the more so, because I had carried it on so long, and had never been taken; for in a word, my new partner in wickedness and I went on together so long, without being ever detected, that we not only grew bold, but we grew rich, and we had at one time one and twenty gold watches in our hands" (202–3). Yet even as Moll deplores her moral condition, a note of irrepressible triumph is heard in those twenty-one gold watches, as her pleasure in remembering her triumphs mixes with tough-minded analysis of her moral failure.

As she herself warns, Moll is "but a very indifferent monitor," and readers are advised to construct their "own just reflections, which they will be more able to make effectual than I, who so soon forget myself" (126). At the very end of her story, Moll wonders at the goodness of Providence, and the abhorrence of her past such wonder provokes, but breaks off the reflection: "I leave the reader to improve these thoughts, as no doubt they will see cause, and I go on to the fact" (337). Characteristically, Moll is a sort of ironic chorus on the foolishness she has seen in her time, and her discourse is peppered with wry reflections. Women who run into marriage, for example, "are a sort of ladies that are to be pray'd for among the rest of distemper'd people; and to me they look like people that venture their whole estates in a lottery where there is a hundred thousand blanks to one prize" (75). And Moll the underworld moralist views some of her old associates with compact sarcasm. She remembers with some distaste two thieves, a man and a woman, with whom she worked briefly. Clumsy and coarse in their larcenous techniques, they are caught in housebreaking, which Moll always avoids, and her sardonic summary reveals her own sense of propriety: "they were partners it seems in the trade they carried on; and partners in something else too. In short, they robb'd together, lay together, were taken together, and at last were hang'd together" (208–9).

In other words, *Moll Flanders* is not the conventionally defiant and/or repentant criminal of popular biography but possesses a distinctive, individuated voice and a crafty intelligence. She sounds at times like the former pickpocket she is, speaking in a racy demotic style, capable of self-irony, double entendre, and word play. As Defoe arranges it, she is an old woman looking back on her life with complicated retrospection, repentant of course but also undiminished in wit and spirit and in fact pretty satisfied with a good deal of her story. The reader is conscious, in effect, of two characters, one narrating, the other acting. Much of Defoe's specifically novelistic innovation in *Moll Flanders* lies in just this process of interpretation old Moll brings to her narrative. What we are reading is not simply a record of a character in action but a process of remembering and interpreting that action whereby character is revealed and developed in complex ways through the act of narration itself. Moreover, many of Moll's interpretations of her life as she narrates it are open to question, morally inconsistent and thereby revealing (like the mixture of pride and repentance noted above) but also endearingly human. To an important extent, this tendency to ethical neutrality is the result of Defoe's realism which, as Ian Watt notes, subordinates "any coherent ulterior significance to the illusion that the text represents the authentic lucubrations of an historical person."[17]

But this ethically neutral realism is accompanied, as always in Defoe's fictions, by elaborate didactic claims. The preface stresses that this is an expurgated autobiography, with Moll's saltier language cleaned up and "some of the vicious part of her life, which cou'd not be modestly told," left out (2). In spite of what it calls the book's "infinite variety," the preface claims that everything in it conforms to poetic justice: "there is not a wicked action in any part of it, but is first or last rendered unhappy and unfortunate: There is not a superlative villain brought upon the stage, but either he is brought to an unhappy end, or brought to be a penitent" (3). The book is also, says the preface, a warning and an inspiration. Reading about Moll's criminal techniques will help honest people to beware of such thieves, and watching her "application to a sober life, and industrious management at last in Virginia" will teach the reader that "no case can be so low, so despicable, or so empty of prospect, but that an unwearied industry will go a great way to deliver us from it, will in time raise the meanest creature to appear again in the world, and give him a new cast for his life" (4).

Whether Defoe wrote this preface is uncertain. But its promises of different satisfactions for readers of *Moll Flanders* point to the book's perennially fascinating ambiguities. As some recent critics have insisted, *Moll Flanders* is best understood, like *Robinson Crusoe,* as a version of spiritual autobiography, depicting in Moll a process of spiritual "hard-

ening" dramatically resolved by her true repentance in Newgate. For
G. A. Starr, the scattered, episodic quality of the narrative is unified
by "a gradual, fairly systematic development of the heroine's spiritual
condition."[18] As she reviews her life of crime, Moll presents its roots
in economic necessity and urges readers to remember "that a time of
distress is a time of dreadful temptation, and all the strength to resist
is taken away; poverty presses, the soul is made desperate by distress,
and what can be done?" (191). But mysterious forces cooperate with
economic factors, and it is the devil who lays snares, who leaves on
the counter top the unattended bundle that is Moll's first theft, who
whispers in her ear, "take the bundle; be quick; do it this moment"
(191). Moll renders vividly her guilty fear and remorse after this initial
theft, but "an evil counsellor within" pushes her on. Coming upon a
child wearing a costly necklace, Moll leads her into an alley and is
tempted to kill the child after lifting the jewelry: "Here, I say, the
Devil put me upon killing the child in the dark alley, that it might
not cry; but the very thought frighted me so that I was ready to drop
down" (194). The inner life Moll shows us has its darkly mysterious
side, and this hastily suppressed glimpse of homicidal possibility suggests
that her will for survival is instinctively ruthless.

Defoe seems to be marking the limits of self-knowledge and social
and economic determinants, which can only explain so much. Temptations
like these and Moll's subsequent settling into a criminal life illustrate
progressive spiritual and moral decay and identify the narrative for some
critics as spiritual autobiography. For other readers, Moll seems to
embody an irrepressible individualism rather like Defoe's and to affirm
the possibilities of triumphant survival in a hostile modern environment.
Strictly speaking, these critical views are not opposed but describe the
two different levels on which Defoe's book operates. Defoe clearly
intended, however unsystematically, to portray Moll's life according to
the Christian pattern of sin and repentance. Various factors, not the
least of which may have been the haste with which he worked, made
those intentions operate only fitfully or at least inefficiently and helped
to produce something more like a novel than a spiritual autobiography.

Spiritual autobiography is necessarily single-minded, driving toward
the moment of conversion, sifting experience for evidence of spiritual
evolution or erosion. *Moll Flanders,* from its outset, is distracted from
such Christian intensity by an interest in secular variety and psychological
plenitude, the excitement of extreme situations Defoe's audience clearly
wanted. Moreover, Defoe's characteristic approach involves an almost

consuming curiosity about experience in all its forms that tends to make his autobiographers only intermittently focused on their spiritual development. What Moll delivers most of the time is precisely what later novelists offer more self-consciously: the process whereby an individual gradually develops an identity in relation to society, coming to self-consciousness both within and against an external world, establishing a social self and discovering a private self that may diverge radically from that public identity. As Leo Braudy puts it very forcefully, the peculiar power of Defoe's novels appears to come from his "awakening to the implications of speaking in his own voice or masquerading in the voice of another," in the process grappling "with the problem of individuality and identity with an energy bordering on obsessiveness."[19] With all its clumsiness and inconsistency and to some extent because of them, *Moll Flanders* conjures up a personality, a character claiming quite aggressively to be a unique individual with a history entirely her own, not simply a moral or social type. In / that struggle for individuality, a matter of mere survival at times, an opposing external world is richly revealed, and Defoe's psychological realism is always rooted in a corresponding social realism.

From the beginning, Moll's narrative turns on that revealing struggle. She is born in Newgate prison, as the title page advertises, but her childhood and adolescence are hardly predicted by such birth. What Defoe promises his readers, after all, is something out of the ordinary, so Moll does not become as we might expect part of the urban underclass like Colonel Jack. As far as she can remember, she was kidnapped by gypsies and left at Colchester, in Essex, where she is raised by a poor woman paid by the local parish. When she is fourteen, her "nurse" dies, and she is adopted by an upper middle-class family. In these opening pages Moll is enmeshed in institutions like the rudimentary child welfare system of the time and the upper middle-class family, but she also actively resists their influence, an outsider somehow, different from other foster children in wanting to live by her needle rather than become a servant, precociously if innocently independent, conscious always as she tells us of her social difference even within the bosom of the wealthy family that takes her in. Thus, she absorbs the privileged education the daughters receive without being officially entitled to it: "as I was always with them, I learn'd as fast as they; and tho' the masters were not appointed to teach me, yet I learn'd by imitation and enquiry, all that they learn'd by instruction and direction" (18). By her own account but also she insists by the "opinion of all that knew the family" (19), Moll is the natural superior of these privileged girls: "and in some things, I had the advantage of my ladies, tho' they were my superiors; but they were all the gifts of nature, and which all their fortunes could not furnish" (18).

In other words, Moll's history simultaneously dramatizes social inevitability and the personal freedom that operates to modify its effects. Carried along by circumstances and institutions, she exploits natural gifts that enable her to attract the attention of her adoptive family in the first place. Like all Defoe's heroes, self-made to some extent, she learns by "imitation and enquiry." In a sense, this opening set of events predicts the pattern of the rest of the book. Over and over, in increasingly difficult situations, Moll shows how she ultimately transformed limiting, nearly disastrous circumstances into opportunities for expansion and self-renewal. And yet, *Moll Flanders* is hardly schematic. Moll's early days in Colchester are a turbulent record of sexual awakening and betrayal. Seduced by the elder brother of the house, she is married off in due course to the younger, but before that dull outcome she has her moments of excitement and self-discovery. The exact nature of those moments is worth dwelling on, for they help explain how the book operates on two complementary levels.

Finding Moll alone one day, the elder brother impulsively kisses her and declares his love. Several days later, kissing her more violently on a bed, he gives Moll five guineas, repeating all this shortly after and giving her more gold. Here are Moll's reflections on these events:

It will not be strange, if I now began to think, but alas! it was but with very little solid reflection: I had a most unbounded stock of vanity and pride, and but a very little stock of vertue; I did indeed cast sometimes with myself what my young master aim'd at, but thought of nothing but the fine words, and the gold; whether he intended to marry me, or not to marry me, seem'd a matter of no great consequence to me; nor did my thoughts so much as suggest to me the necessity of making any capitulation [i.e., striking a bargain] for myself, till he came to make a kind of formal proposal to me, as you shall hear presently.

Thus I gave up myself to a readiness of being ruined without the least concern, and am a fair *memento* to all young women, whose vanity prevails over their vertue: Nothing was ever so stupid on both sides, had I acted as became me, and resisted as vertue and honour requir'd, this gentleman had either desisted his attacks, finding no room to expect the accomplishment of his design, or had made fair, and honourable proposals of marriage; in which case, whoever had blam'd him, no body could have blam'd me. In short, if he had known me, and how easy the trifle he aim'd at, was to be had, he would have troubled his head no farther, but have given me four or five guineas, and have lain with me the next time he had come at me; and if I had known his thoughts, and how hard he thought I would be to be gain'd, I might have made my own terms with him; and if I had not capitulated for an immediate marriage, I might for a maintenance till marriage, and might have had what I would; for he was already rich to excess, besides what he had in expectation; but I seem'd wholly to have abandoned all such thoughts as these, and was taken up onely with the pride of my beauty, and of being belov'd by such a gentleman; as for the gold I spent whole hours in looking upon it; I told [i.e., counted] the guineas over and over a thousand times a day. (25–26)

Highlighted here is the gap between Moll the actor and Moll the narrator. In her ironic, slightly brutal assessment of her young innocence, Moll reveals how she has changed since then, substituted a strategically precise (and coldly calculating) knowledge of human relationships for the spontaneous emotions and passionate involvement of her youth. And yet Moll is divided in the attitudes she projects, concerned about underlining the moral of her story, an illustration of vanity overcoming virtue, but revealing in her actual narrative mainly a disgust with her naiveté rather than any moral regret. In the second paragraph, the relative formality and moral conclusiveness of the first sentence slide into the colloquial outburst "Nothing was ever so stupid on both sides." Moll outlines a self-protective, legalistic approach to human relationships. The ideal course would have been not so much moral as blamelessly advantageous: "whoever had blam'd him, no body could have blam'd me." In a crucial metaphor in the first paragraph, Moll speaks of her small "stock" of virtue and her huge "stock" of vanity and pride. The expression seems conventional enough here, but as the book proceeds the reader will see how Moll's moral and psychological reflections are governed by the mercantile materialism implicit in "stock." Her story turns on the problems of accumulating capital; her personality is formed in terms of assets and liabilities. And in fact as Moll remembers it, what thrilled her chiefly about the elder brother's advances was not the sex, hastily summarized, but the gold obsessively, erotically counted. As Defoe masterfully arranges it, young Moll's passion is compounded of various forms of excitement; her sexuality is inseparable from the thrilling prospect of money and social advancement. In fact, the scene's erotic center is Moll counting the gold over and over again, realizing instinctively the deeply sexual resonances of money and its power. To be sure, old Moll sees only the latter and disparages the sexual ("the trifle he aim'd at"), thus beginning a consistent and unifying refrain in the narrative.

In much Western literature, what often identifies female characters is a turbulent, compulsive sexuality. Granted a richer emotional life than men by a persistent patriarchal myth, women are both exalted and degraded in this sexual division of psychological labor. Their inner life can make them the moral superiors of men, more sensitive, caring and so on, but their emotional sensitivity frequently renders them sexually unstable, in early eighteenth-century drama and fiction quite often the victims of self-destructive romantic passion. One recent commentator on *Moll Flanders* explains this situation in economic terms. Excluded from meaningful economic activity by early modern capitalism, women "were endowed with a moral superiority to compensate for their economic diminution."[20] What is striking about Defoe's version of this myth is his subversion of it. After this initial, in some ways quite conventional seduction by the elder brother (the sexual exploitation of servants and lower-class women by upper-class men was a popular literary subject as well as a social reality), Moll quickly acquires a cooler, infinitely more controlled personality, bent upon survival and prosperity, out to use sexuality as a means to those ends, no longer the helpless prey of her emotions. At least, that is what old Moll quickly jumps to in her narrative, the hasty summarizing of her next five years married to Robin, the younger brother, pointing to her impatience with a discarded younger self. "It concerns the story in hand very little, to enter into the farther particulars of the family, or of myself, for the five years that I liv'd with this husband; only to observe that I had two children by him, and that at the end of five year he died" (58). Instead, Moll provides the first of what will be regular accountings of her financial condition. Only moderately profitable is her comment on this marriage's bottom line: "nor was I much mended by the match: Indeed I had preserv'd the elder brother's bonds to me, to pay me 500£ which he offer'd me for my consent to marry his brother; and with this and what I had saved of the money he formerly gave me, and about as much more by my husband, left me a widow with about 1200£ in my pocket" (58).

Moll now embarks on a tangled set of adventures, in all of which her object is to marry profitably: "I had been trick'd once by *that cheat call'd* LOVE, but the game was over; I was resolv'd now to be married, or nothing, and to be well married, or not at all" (60).

Experience soon teaches her that in London marriages were "the consequences of politick schemes, for forming interests, and carrying on business, and that LOVE had no share, or but very little in the matter" (67). In much of what follows, Defoe displays his characteristic fascination with duplicity and manipulation of others. In sequences too complicated for extensive summary, Moll learns to hold herself in reserve, to assume false names, to pretend to fortune in order to attract men, and in general to adapt her identity for self-advantage. What matters, above all, is self-control, keeping her true self secret and essentially apart, at least from men. A good half of the novel is, in fact, devoted to these adventures, which result in five sexual relationships, four of them marriages, one of them incestuous and one of them bigamous. The abilities Moll quickly acquires to manage these relationships have seemed to many readers to be fairly implausible if interesting in their obvious affinities with Defoe's own talents. The marriage market where Moll wheels and deals is not essentially different from markets Defoe knew at first hand, and Moll's conspiratorial alliances with other women in her campaigns to bag suitable husbands echo the political maneuvers in which he was still involved.

And yet Defoe's own published opinions about marriage were very far from Moll's calculating materialism. *Conjugal Lewdness; or Matrimonial Whoredom. A Treatise concerning the Use and Abuse of the Marriage Bed* (1727) is as eloquent in its praise of marriage as it is fiery in its denunciations of sexual and mercenary motives for entering into it. Defoe counsels caution, warning against the hell of an unhappy marriage: "HOUSHOLD strife is a terrestrial Hell, at least, 'tis an emblem of real Hell." But he also labels marriage the summation of "all that can be called happy in the life of man."[21] Clearly, *Moll Flanders* provided an opportunity to imagine a subversive marginality otherwise unavailable to Defoe. An insolated and embattled woman like Moll is to some extent a metaphor for that marginality rather than a plausible version of reality, her experience in the marriage market, like her criminal career afterwards, serving as a means for exploring normally forbidden possibilities of action and self-consciousness and perhaps for enjoying the play of strategy and counter-strategy, as well as the exhilaration of impersonation and social movement that are so important in Defoe's own personality.

But some critics contend that moral irony governs the book, that Defoe intended his readers to see Moll's views on marriage as abhorrent and to realize that Moll is inconsistent, untrue to the self-serving materialism she claims to live by. The case to be made for this reading is a good one. Even old Moll has to admit that she was not immune to lingering traces of passion. While she lived with her first husband, the younger brother of her seducer, 'I never was in bed with my husband, but I wish'd my self in the arms of his brother . . . I committed adultery and incest with him every day in my desires" (59). By her own admission, Moll is frequently for all her tough talk betrayed by her emotions. First, she is "hurried on (by my fancy to a gentleman)" (61) to marry her second husband, the shopkeeper who goes bankrupt and deserts her. Later, at Bath she becomes a wealthy man's mistress and her moral qualms are stilled by growing affection: "But these were thoughts of no weight, and whenever he came to me they vanish'd; for his company was so delightful, that there was no being melancholly when he was there" (120). In similar fashion, Moll later agrees to marry the banker who has just divorced his unfaithful wife and proposed to her, but she is struck by sudden guilt. He little knows, she exclaims, that he is divorcing one whore to marry another, "that has lain with thirteen men, and has had a child since he saw me" (182). Her resolution would warm the heart of the most sentimental women's magazine reader: "I'll be a true wife to him, and love him suitably to the strange excess of his passion for me; I will make him amends, if possible, by what he shall see, for the cheats and abuses I put upon him, which he does not see" (182). Finally, Moll's most elaborate scheme for mercenary marriage collapses comically when she discovers that the new husband she thought was a rich Irish peer is a penniless fortune hunter. But when he leaves her the next day, her reaction is intense: "I eat but little, and after dinner I fell into a vehement fit of crying, every now and then, calling him by his name, which was James, O Jemy! said I, come back, come back, I'll give you all I have; I'll beg, I'll starve with you, and thus I run raving about the room several times" (153).

Although there are times when Moll sounds like a female impersonator, she acquires skills at survival and manipulation by painfully repressing emotions that the book identifies as specifically female susceptibilities. At the least, Defoe tries to arrange a balance between the emotional melodrama that gives Moll's life shape and the artful manipulations by which she survives those psychological crises. Sometimes, he clearly falters in the attempt, and long stretches of Moll's marital career are really fascinated expositions of her cleverness as a sort of confidence woman, a skilled predator in the sexual jungle. "I play'd with this lover," she says and repeats an earlier image, "as an angler does with a trout: I found I had him fast on the hook, so I jested with his new proposal; and put him off" (140). And yet as events show, Moll is herself being tricked and played with, by some of her male antagonists and ultimately by fate. Thanks to the disasters that follow Moll's manipulations and her own confessions of emotional vulnerability, a personality emerges rather different from the one Moll herself projects.

As the title page luridly advertises, Moll commits incest. But her marriage to the man who turns out to be her brother is the culmination of her first really elaborate and successful marital scheme. With the help of her female friend, a sea captain's wife, the first in a series of crucial female accomplices for Moll, she passes for a woman of fortune and attracts a number of suitors: "I who had a subtile game to play, had nothing now to do but to single out from them all the properest man that might be for my purpose; that is to say, the man who was most likely to depend upon the hear say of a fortune, and not enquire too far into the particulars; and unless I did this, I did nothing, for my case would not bear much enquiry" (78). Even as Moll assumes an identity and undermines any sort of sincerity by her evasions and manipulations, she is ironically discovering an unlooked for biological identity, being cruelly manipulated by fate or at least by coincidence. Moreover, once she learns, in Virginia where she has gone to live with her new husband, that her mother-in-law is her mother and her husband her brother, the secrecy that she has chosen as a means of power is transformed into a hell of private anguish. "I resolv'd, that it was absolutely necessary to conceal it all, and not make the least discovery of it either to mother or husband; and thus I liv'd with the greatest pressure imaginable for three year more, but had no more children" (89).

Moll's implausible resilience allows her to return to England hardly the worse for wear and to pick up her career as woman on the make. Defoe is not novelist enough to render the cumulative effects of emotional stress. What he does try to do some justice to is the coexistence in Moll of contradictory elements of controlling calculation and compelling emotion. Moll's life is at once a series of free choices and coercive circumstances, an attempt to balance various kinds of necessity, biological and social, with personal freedom. That attempt comes to a head in Moll's arrest and incarceration in Newgate prison, the most moving and significant sequence in the novel.

After several close calls in her fantastically successful career as a thief, Moll is finally caught in the act and with no real transition the episodic rush of narrative, with its high-spirited accumulation of tricks and disguises and its panorama of scenes and faces, slows to a melodramatic halt. Moll is, as she says, "fix'd indeed" (273), for her narrative is suddenly restricted to one terrible location and the expansive forward movement of her criminal career is now shifted violently back to the past and the fate it has apparently fixed for her. Moll's narrative habits so far consist mainly of sketching her movements and rendering dialogue, giving us people and their interaction rather than the places they inhabit. What matters to her story are strategies and states of mind, and even exotic places like Virginia remain indistinct, mere stage backdrops. Unlike the London streets of her criminal career, which are diagramed to give the reader a sense of the swiftness and agility of Moll's movements, Newgate is solid rock, looming gigantically as a place of confinement, a palpable set of walls and an embodiment of inescapable, immovable circumstances. For almost the first time in her narrative, Moll attempts to describe a physical location, sliding from the fearful insight that she was destined for it, to a still half-boastful reminder of her skill in avoiding it, to her unique admission of its fateful force.

I was carried to *Newgate;* that horrid place! my very blood chills at the mention of its name; the place, where so many of my comrades had been lock'd up, and from whence they went to the fatal tree [i.e., the gallows]; the place where my mother suffered so deeply, where I was brought into the world, and from whence I expected no redemption, but by an infamous death: To conclude, the place that had so long expected me, and which with so much art and success I had so long avoided. I was now fix'd indeed; 'tis impossible to describe the terror of my mind, when I was first brought in, and when I look'd round upon all the horrors of that dismal place: I look'd on myself as lost, and that I had nothing to think of, but of going out of the world, and that with the utmost infamy; the hellish noise, the roaring, swearing and clamour, the stench and nastiness, and all the dreadful croud of afflicting things that I saw there; joyn'd together to make the place seem an emblem of hell itself, and a kind of an entrance into it. (273–74)

And yet that is hardly the worst aspect of Newgate, since Moll's (or Defoe's) powers of physical evocation are not great. Moll is plunged into fear and trembling and thinks night and day "of gibbets and halters, evil spirits and devils . . . harrass'd between the dreadful apprehensions of death, and the terror of my conscience reproaching

me with my past horrible life" (277). But what Moll describes at
greater length than this terror is the transformation that follows and
cancels it. Heretofore, Moll has evaded the full consequences of her
circumstances; her story is a testimonial to the powers of individualistic
self-creation. But Newgate operates as the concentrated essence of an
irresistible external world that erodes free will and individual agency,
that determines personality and destroys freedom. In an unusually vivid
image for the plainspoken Moll, she evokes the prison's compelling
force. It operates "like the waters in the caveties, and hollows of
mountains, which petrifies and turns into stone whatever they are suffer'd
to drop upon," so her confinement in this enforced environment turns
her "first stupid and senseless, then brutish and thoughtless, and at last
raving mad" (278). Moll is transformed, loses the identity she thought
she had: "I scarce retain'd the habit and custom of good breeding and
manners, which all along till now run thro' my conversation; so thoro'
a degeneracy had possess'd me, that I was no more the same thing
that I had been, than if I had never been otherwise than what I was
now" (279).

In the context of Defoe's fiction, this is a crucial moment. All his
narratives challenge the notion of simple or stable identity. His characters
record nothing less than the fluid and dynamic nature of personality,
a matter of changing roles, wearing masks, responding to circumstances,
and discovering new possibilities of self-expression. Up to now, Moll
has defined herself by evading the restraint built into the idea of simple
identity. Both as woman and as criminal, her survival has been a matter
of reserving the truth about herself; and her identity, if she can be said
to have any, lies in those repeated acts of deception and self-reservation.
Those acts seem in stark contrast to this involuntary transformation into
what Moll calls a "meer Newgate-Bird" (279). But Defoe may have
intended a profound irony. Without realizing it, Moll's immersion in
crime past the point of necessity has "hardened" her in vice, slowly
transformed her and eroded her powers of moral choice. Newgate is
simply the culmination of that process, an accelerated revelation of the
real Moll formed by a life of crime, "harden'd" in a sort of moral
stupor long before she arrived in Newgate.

There are two events that restore Moll to self-consciousness. One, of
course, is her spiritual conversion, the true repentance that is the climax
of her spiritual autobiography. Condemned to death, Moll is visited by
a minister who leads her to regret her past out of more than fear of
earthly punishment. Responding to his prayers and entreaties, Moll

repents out of concern for having offended God, conscious as never before of her eternal welfare. The experience, Moll admits, is impossible to render, just as the minister's methods and reasonings are beyond her powers of narration: "I am not able to repeat the excellent discourses of this extraordinary man; 'tis all that I am able to do to say, that he reviv'd my heart, and brought me into such a condition, that I never knew any thing in my life before: I was cover'd with shame and tears for things past, and yet had at the same time a secret surprizing joy at the prospect of being a true penitent" (289). Moll, once again, leaves it to "the work of every sober reader to make just reflections" upon her religious conversion; she is "not mistress of words enough to express them" (288). What she is able to describe very precisely is the other event that brings her out of her lethargy, the arrival in Newgate of her Lancashire husband, Jemy, along with two other captured highwaymen. Overwhelmed with grief for him, she tells us, Moll blames herself for his taking to a life of crime, and the result is a return to self-consciousness: "I bewail'd his misfortunes, and the ruin he was now come to, at such a rate, that I relish'd nothing now, as I did before, and the first reflections I made upon the horrid detestable life I had liv'd, began to return upon me, and as these things return'd my abhorrence of the place I was in, and of the way of living in it, return'd also; in a word, I was perfectly chang'd, and became another body" (281). "Conscious guilt," as Moll calls it, restores her to herself, to what she calls the "thinking" that equals self-consciousness. "I began to think, and to think is one real advance from hell to heaven; all that hellish harden'd state and temper of soul . . . is but a deprivation of thought; he that is restor'd to his power of thinking is restor'd to himself" (281).

This self-restoration precedes the spiritual conversion and is in effect a precondition for true repentance. Moll is restored to herself, we can say, by regaining her sense that she can exercise a controlling relationship with other people, and her rather (on the face of it) overstated guilt about Jemy marks the beginning of a revivifying connection with her past. As the last phase of her career begins, Moll resonstructs certain aspects of her past, no longer plunging ahead from episode to episode and improvising survival as she goes but revisiting and reintegrating past and present. Reprieved from execution and ordered "transported" to Virginia, she persuades the reluctant Jemy to come along and settles in Virginia with the help of carefully enumerated assets accumulated in her life of crime. Once there, she buys her freedom and establishes herself and Jemy as proprietors of a plantation, increasing her holdings when she discovers that her mother has died and left her an inheritance. This last she discovers by seeking out, in disguise, the son—Humphry, who is now a grown man—she had with her brother-husband. The scene when she first glimpses her son is a fine moment but raises again the recurrent problem of psychological realism. When someone points Humphry out to her, Moll is deeply affected:

you may guess, if you can, what a confus'd mixture of joy and fright possest my thoughts upon this occasion, for I immediately knew that this was no body else, but my own son . . . let any mother of children that reads this, consider it, and but think with what anguish of mind I restrain'd myself; what yearnings of soul I had in me to embrace him, and weep over him; and how I thought all my entrails turn'd within me, that my very bowels mov'd, and I knew not what to do; as I now know not how to express those agonies: When he went from me I stood gazing and trembling, and looking after him as long as I could see him; then sitting down on the grass, just at a place I had mark'd, I made as if I lay down to rest me, but turn'd from her [the woman who has identified Moll's son], and lying on my face wept, and kiss'd the ground that he had set his foot on. (321–22)

By itself, this is convincing, especially in the care with which Moll disguises herself and hides her intense emotions, preserving something of her old cunning at self-concealment even as she reveals herself to the reader. But within the context of Moll's career as a mother in which she has more or less abandoned or carelessly disposed of a string of children such intensity may seem strangely inconsistent at best. And yet without giving Defoe more credit for novelistic sophistication than he deserves, the scene fits exactly into this last phase of Moll's career. Moll's intensity is a coherent reaction to her own maternal failures, and Humphry represents accumulated guilt as well as inexpressible joy. Moreover, the scene begins yet another sequence in which Moll can operate in her characteristically self-renewing way. As so often before, she has a secret and acquires a confidant to manipulate the secret to advantage. Only now her collaborator is her son and the secret links her joyfully and productively with a past rather than just concealing it. As she and Humphry huddle together and he hands over Moll's substantial inheritance, she looks up "with great thankfulness to the hand of Providence, which had done such wonders for me, who had been myself the greatest wonder of wickedness, perhaps that had been suffered to live in the world" (336–37). The moral ambiguity in Moll's thanksgiving, with its irrepressible self-promotion, is a link with the unrepentant Moll of earlier times. For some readers, this particular inconsistency and adamant inability to become simply moral types are what make Defoe's characters a uniquely living collection.

Chapter Six
Narrative to Novel: *Roxana*

Perhaps the most disturbing example of the moral ambiguity that seems to be at the center of Defoe's fiction occurs in his last novel, *Roxana* (1724), which is on several counts his most interesting narrative and, as Maximillian E. Novak remarks, "both morally and artistically his most complex work."[1] Like *Moll Flanders,* however, *Roxana* has its roots in popular narrative, as its full title discloses: *The Fortunate Mistress; or, a History of the life and vast variety of fortunes of Mademoiselle de Beleau, afterwards call'd the Countess de Wintselsheim, in Germany. Being the person known by the name of the Lady Roxana in the time of King Charles II.* Defoe's title in fact deliberately echoes that of one of Eliza Haywood's novellas published the previous year, *Idalia: or, the Unfortunate Mistress* (1723), and calls to mind the titles of other popular tales of passion and betrayal, steamy soft-core romances such as Haywood was then producing. By the mention of Charles II in his title, Defoe aligns the book with secret histories or scandal chronicles, bestselling, trashy collections of amorous and political intrigues in high places best exemplified by Delarivière Manley's immensely popular *Secret Memoirs and Manners of several Persons of Quality, of both Sexes. From the New Atalantis, an island in the Mediterranean* (1709).

Roxana's resemblance to these books is in actuality superficial. As Ian Bell points out, Defoe and his publisher were clearly attempting to cash in on the popularity of these two forms, the erotic novella and the secret history, by combining them in a novel way, mainly by a much more careful verisimilitude and historical particularity. The result transforms these two vulgar narrative types into something far more complex, both a political and moral satire and an intensely personal confession.[2] But the satire is entirely up to the moral judgment of the reader. Roxana tells her own story, and like Moll Flanders she has a wicked and withering intelligence with its own powerfully satiric insights into male privilege. Defoe gives her a sort of proto-feminist sensibility, which he then seems to undercut by dramatizing its distorting excesses. This satire cuts both ways.

But the satire that modern scholars have pointed to is rooted in the history of the times and would probably have been crystal clear to a contemporary reader. David Blewett explains that Roxana has two opposing modes of existence, one spatial and the other temporal, and these are essential to the book's social satire. As a successful courtesan, Roxana eventually acquires an apartment in Pall Mall, in the fashionable West End of London where the king and the court live; but when she gives all that up, she goes to live quietly at the other side of town, "the City," home of tradesmen, shopkeepers, and bankers, where Defoe himself was born. In similar fashion, in Europe Roxana is the mistress of a German prince in the service of Louis XIV in Paris, but she later marries a Dutch merchant, who has courted her for years, and lives respectably (at least on the surface) with him in Holland. For contemporary English readers, these were not neutral locations. Paris was traditionally associated with that moral laxity and sensuality the English perennially ascribe to the French, and it was also the seat of French tyranny, a refuge for the exiled house of Stuart and thereby an embodiment of potential danger for English political stability and power. Holland, on the other hand, was a sober trading nation like England, a commercial rival but a political ally, and also the home of the late William III, Defoe's hero.[3]

The temporal aspect of the satire looks at first like one of the many examples of Defoe's carelessness. Roxana drops hints that she served as one of Charles II's mistresses, and yet Defoe dates events precisely so that she would have been twelve years old in 1685 when that monarch died. The book is clearly set during the reign of George I but also evokes just as clearly the world of the dissolute Restoration court surrounding Charles II. Modern critics have rescued Defoe from traditional charges of clumsiness by calling this a deliberately double and satirically effective time scheme.[4] In Blewett's words, Defoe thus satirizes his own time by "drawing a moral comparison" between the two eras.[5]

Roxana herself is part of these satiric targets, deeply implicated in those worlds and thereby committed to the false values Defoe is attacking. And yet the very fact of first-person narration makes all this less than certain or at least unfocused. Although it seems clear, as G. A. Starr remarks, that Defoe intended to "consign Roxana to the devil," to depict her as nothing less by the end of the book than a soul in despair, she communicates a strength of will, clarity of purpose, and worldly efficiency that make her a fascinating if not always admirable personality.[6] Unlike the cartoonlike characters, examples of swooning and seduced female innocence, featured in amatory novellas, and unlike the monsters of vice and corruption who inhabit scandal chronicles such as Manley's *New Atalantis,* Roxana displays psychological depth and complexity. A simple reaction to her seems out of the question. Like all Defoe's autobiographers, she draws readers into a sort of admiring identification with her struggle to survive and prosper against the odds. With increasing skill, intelligence, and undeniable candor about her own moral responsibility, Roxana evokes much more clearly than Moll Flanders or Colonel Jack the psychological consequences of amoral survival in a world of unforgiving economic circumstances.

Solidly middle class, the daughter of well-to-do French Protestant refugees to England, Roxana finds herself at the desperate edge when her first husband deserts her. In spite of the melodramatic events she begins with, Roxana establishes herself from the first as the most racy and energetic of Defoe's narrators. The voice we hear is of a somewhat world-weary, sophisticated courtesan, given to sexual double entendre and cynically knowing analysis of sex and power. At times, she seems an effectively androgynous character ("a *man-woman,*" as she later calls herself) who has overcome what she depicts as an oppressively male-dominated society. When she learns years later of the death of her first husband, Roxana is hardly eager to remarry. She knows, as Blewett points out, that an unmarried woman has the same rights as a man but loses them when she marries and becomes in the legal parlance of the time "a *feme covert,*" whose legal status depends on that of her husband.[7] Defoe himself wrote about the abuses thus licensed when he remarked that a wife should be more than a servant, that in matrimony "the obligation is reciprocal, 'tis drawing in an equal yoke; love knows no superior or inferior, no imperious command on one hand, no reluctant subjection on the other."[8] In refusing to become merely "an upper-servant" (170) and preferring the independence of a mistress, however, Roxana takes Defoe's liberal opinions dangerously far, talking what one of her lovers calls "a kind of Amazonian language" (212).

Like this bewildered lover, readers, especially nowadays, may wonder just what to make of Roxana's stirring feminism, which coincides with some of Defoe's own opinions. As early as the 1697 *Essay upon Projects,* Defoe had criticized conventional restrictions on women, calling there for the foundation of "An Academy for Women." One of his comments in this proposal anticipates his strong-minded heroines: "what they might be capable of being bred to, is plain from some instances of female wit, which this age is not without; which upbraids us with injustice, and looks as if we denied women the advantages of education, for fear they should vye with the men in their improvements."[9] Roxana tells us that she went to English schools, but the only accomplishment she dwells on is her singing and dancing: "I danc'd, as some say, naturally, lov'd it extremely, and sung well also" (39). But her real education begins after her disastrous marriage, at fifteen, to a well-to-do merchant, "an eminent brewer" (39).

Like Moll Flanders, Roxana warns female readers about the dangers of marriage in a world dominated by fools of the opposite sex, and Defoe seems at first glance to be using her as a sort of mouthpiece or persona for his own forthright opinions on the consequences of ill-considered marriages. As he wrote a few years later, hasty marriage is a foretaste of hell: "the strife breaks out insensibly; the contention, the contradiction, and all the little thwartings and waspishness, which lay the foundation of eternal discord; these all, like weeds, grow and spread under the decaying plant called love, till at last they check and smother it entirely, and leave the family a kind of hell in miniature."[10] Roxana's hell comes after her first husband deserts her, and in her summation of it the situation seems almost comic. "Never, ladies, marry a fool," she warns, for "with another husband you *may,* I say, be unhappy, but with a fool you *must*" (40). Roxana's account of her eight years "with this thing call'd a husband" (39) is retrospectively knowing and sexually sophisticated. Careless and inefficient in his trade as a brewer (like the case histories Defoe described the next year in *The Complete English Tradesman* [1725]), her husband does heed Roxana's warnings to withdraw from business to avoid bankruptcy. "I was willing he should draw out while he had something left, lest I should come to be stript at home, and be turn'd out of doors with my children; for I had now five children by him; the only work (perhaps) that fools are good for" (43). But he proves feckless, infatuated with hunting and social appearances until all their capital is gone: "like one stupid, he went on, not valuing all that tears and lamentations could be suppos'd to do; nor did he abate his figure or equipage, his horses or servants, even to the last, till he had not a hundred pound left in the whole world" (43). In due course, however, Roxana achieves her foolish husband's social ambition by sound financial management.

As a successful courtesan, Roxana not only becomes wealthy but plans her financial future shrewdly through investments advised by Sir Robert Clayton (an actual seventeenth-century financier and politician).

This planning and self-management look odd next to the tragic remorse that comes to dominate the book. But Roxana's independence, marital and financial, has to be seen in two qualifying contexts, one external to the narrative, the other part and parcel of it. Defoe's own opinions on various matters are scattered through all his fiction. For example, the Dutch merchant's reply to Roxana's scornful description of married slavery is essentially what Defoe recommends in *Conjugal Lewdness:* "where there was a mutual love, there cou'd be no bondage; but that there was but one interest; one aim; one design; and all conspir'd to make them both very happy" (189). In Defoe's eyes, Blewett points out, Sir Robert Clayton was a shady dealer and the high interest he promises Roxana would have been seen as suspect by Defoe's readers.[11]

More relevant to an assessment of Defoe's skill as a writer, however, is the context Roxana herself presents. "Where had I liv'd? And what dreadful families had I liv'd among, that had frighted me into such terrible apprehensions of things?" (190) asks the Dutch merchant after Roxana declares her independence. The point for readers, underlined by Roxana herself, is that her opinions are derived from her painful experience and express her own pride and vanity. Looking back, Roxana sees her rejection of the merchant's offer of marriage as "the most preposterous thing that ever woman did" (197). Blinded, she goes on to say, by her own vanity, Roxana turns her own sharp scorn upon her past self: "I am a memorial to all that shall read my story; a standing monument of the madness and distraction which pride and infatuations from Hell runs us into; how ill our passions guide us; and how dangerously we act, when we follow the dictates of an ambitious mind" (201). Whatever intellectual validity Roxana's subversive notions may have is completely subordinated, in her own narration, to their function as expressions of her tortured personality. Defoe could not help making her an attractive and powerful character, but he also managed to make her a uniquely self-conscious and revealingly honest figure, painfully aware as she reviews her life of how events drove her on and shaped her opinions and decisions.

Just as in *Moll Flanders,* Defoe makes the reader conscious of the gap between narrator and actor, but the space between the two seems narrower here. A competent and confident narrator, Roxana pulls no punches about her early disasters and the emotional and moral confusion into which she was plunged. From the beginning, Roxana is affected by a fitful sort of moral self-loathing, and her commentary on her past has an analytic penetration that Moll sorely lacks. Roxana reaches for an intensity Moll is incapable of, as she seeks to render internal torments that from the first "thrust in sighs into the middle of all my songs" (83) and during her later, even guiltier years "there was a dart struck into the liver; there was a secret Hell within" (305). Even as she strives to communicate the emotions that accompanied them, Roxana is always crystal clear about the facts of her case. For example, she surrounds her initial fall into sexual immorality with the full complexity of circumstances, both external and internal.

Roxana pictures herself "in rags and dirt," her house "stripp'd and naked, most of the goods having been seiz'd by the landlord for rent, or sold to buy necessaries; in a word, all was misery and distress, the face of ruin was every where to be seen; we had eaten up almost every thing, and little remain'd, unless, like one of the pitiful women of Jerusalem, I should eat up my very children themselves" (50–51). When her aunt comes to see her, Roxana is sitting on the ground, "with a great heap of old rags, linnen, and other things" (50), looking for things to pawn. Her faithful maid, Amy, enters at this point with "a small breast of mutton, and two great bunches of turnips" (51), a dinner bought by pawning a silver spoon. Roxana, in short, is as circumstantial and detailed about poverty and despair as she is about riches and power later on. Defoe, moreover, makes this scene an integral part of the novel's structure and a coherent backdrop for Roxana's subsequent career. These rags and this stripped-down, starving disorder predict Roxana's drive for fashionable fullness; the graceless heap on the floor is the negative balance for her subsequent triumphant dances in glittering costumes. Evoking her physical hunger, Roxana points by her choice of figurative language to the emotional truth of her career. She will become a devouring female, in the end sacrificing at least one of her children. From her readers, Roxana has nothing to hide, and for attentive readers, she reveals more than she knows.

That frankness extends to her inner life and moral decisions. Moved she says by a mixture of gratitude and sexual attraction, Roxana gives in to her forgiving landlord, who has allowed her to stay on in his house and tries to seduce her. She pleads, like Defoe's other sinners, economic necessity: "poverty was my snare; dreadful poverty! the misery I had been in, was great, such as wou'd make the heart tremble at the apprehensions of its return" (73). But she adds other factors based on self-knowledge: "I was young, handsome, and with all the morti-fications I had met with, was vain, and that not a little; and as it was a new thing, so it was a pleasant thing, to be courted, caress'd, embrac'd, and high professions of affection made by a man so agreeable, and so able to do me good" (73).

Moll has a number of key female allies in her career. Roxana has only Amy, her maid, but their relationship is the most profoundly personal link between two people Defoe ever imagined. A sort of alter ego for Roxana, Amy is an embodied version of Moll's evil counselor within, "a cunning wench, and faithful to me, as the skin to my back" (59), Roxana records in a revealing phrase. Amy articulates what Roxana shies away from. She puts the case for survival at its most brutal, stripping the situation down to elemental necessity, but she also argues persuasively if speciously that circumstances license sexual submission to the kindly but eager landlord. "Your choice is fair and plain; here you may have a handsome, charming gentleman, be rich, live pleasantly, and in plenty; or refuse him, and want a dinner, go in rags, live in tears; in short, beg and starve" (74). More delicately, Amy argues that Roxana is in effect free to marry, her husband having deserted her, and that the landlord is also entitled to marry, his wife having been unfaithful to him and living apart. These and other arguments Amy musters bear out G. A. Starr's thesis that Defoe's novels are organized like cases of conscience, moral dilemmas resolved by the traditional method of "casuistical" analysis. The *Review* featured discussions of such situations as a supplement to the main political material, and the episodic quality of the novels is to some extent the result of Defoe's choosing to focus at length on moments in a life where ethical problems are examined from various points of view. As Starr puts it, "neither natural law, divine law, positive law, nor expediency is a touchstone by which Defoe decides all ethical problems." Rather, Defoe in his own voice in his various writings and through his characters in the fiction "takes up or sets aside each of these sanctions as the occasion demands."[12] The result is that even as *Roxana* records the heroine's moral decay, it testifies to the complexity and force of circumstances, never simply relieving her of blame but dramatizing the difficulty of action and of moral judgment itself.

More completely, perhaps, than in the other novels, the range, curiosity, and sympathy of Defoe's mind are fully on display as he imagines the self-justification and blame that characterize Roxana's review of her past. "Thus Amy and I canvass'd the business between us; the jade prompted the crime, which I had but too much inclination to commit" (75). Roxana, in fact, pointedly rejects casuistical justifications, insisting many times on her own uniquely clear, guilty responsibility. Unlike her landlord,

she "was resolv'd to commit the crime, knowing and owning it to be
a crime" (75). There is a sort of pride in Roxana's reiteration of her
moral precision, sinning "with open eyes," and thereby acquiring "a
double guilt" (78). With her conscience "awake," Roxana sins "knowing
it to be a sin, but having no power to resist." In effect, this is the
only genuinely casuistical moment in the book, since Roxana sees right
away what Moll only dimly understands. Having decided to act against
the dictates of her conscience and bend to the force of terrible circumstances, Roxana is committed to a career of transgressions beyond ordinary
moral restraints: "when this had thus made a hole in my heart, and
I was come to such a height, as to transgress against the light of my
own conscience, I was then fit for any wickedness, and conscience left
off speaking, where it found it cou'd not be heard" (79). A few pages
later, indeed, Roxana provides a memorable illustration of her moral
numbness in a scene that has both horrified and puzzled critics. When
Amy teases her about not being pregnant yet by her landlord, Roxana
forces Amy into bed with him: "Nay, you whore, says I, you said, if
I wou'd put you to-bed, you wou'd with all your heart: and with that,
I sat her down, pull'd off her stockings and shoes, and all her cloaths,
piece by piece, and led her to the bed to him: Here, says I, try what
you can do with your maid" (81). Roxana's brutal point is that all
of them are in the same moral boat, and she presents the scene as
proof "that I had cast off all principle, and all modesty, and had
effectively stifled conscience" (81).

Significantly, Roxana also adds that sexuality had little to do with
it, "for I had nothing of the vice in my constitution; my spirits were
far from being high; my blood had no fire in it, to kindle the flame
of desire" (75). Subsequent events bear out Roxana's claim, since what
follows is a series of sexual manipulations in which she grows progressively
more skilled at exploiting her attractiveness and in which her pleasure
lies in techniques of profitable sexual exploitation rather than in sexuality
itself. In part, Roxana's cold-blooded efficiency as a mistress links her,
as E. Anthony James remarks, with Moll Flanders as a pragmatic trader
in vice.[13] This is not to say that Defoe imagines a moral monster. Most
of Roxana's relationships, as she evokes them, are complicated by
affectionate involvement as well as by profitable manipulation. For
example, when her landlord lover (a jeweler by trade) is killed by
bandits in France, her grief is convincingly extravagant: "I think I
almost cry'd myself to death for him; for I abandon'd myself to all
the excesses of grief; and indeed, I lov'd him to a degree inexpressible"

(89). Defoe's originality lies precisely in Roxana's oscillations and defining inconsistencies as she relives her life in the telling of it. Her story has an eddying motion in which regret and repentance pull her down even as pleasure and affluence bear her up. And yet, *Roxana* is more than a whirlpool of episodes and incidents. It has a narrative pattern, a unified plot more coherent than Defoe had ever managed.

That coherence is best illustrated by looking at two sequences, which in the end are crucially linked. In the first of these, Roxana acquires her name and scores her greatest triumph. Having served happily and profitably as the mistress of a German prince at Paris and after refusing her Dutch merchant's marriage proposal, Roxana establishes herself in the fashionable part of London, where she is pursued by many "lovers, beaus, and fops of quality" (212). But her sights are set higher, and "nothing less than the King himself was in my eye" (212). One night she gives a ball, at which arrive some masked courtiers among whom, as she guesses, is the king. What follows needs to be quoted at length. Roxana dresses herself in a Turkish costume, purchased during her stay in Italy with the prince and here meticulously described:

The dress was extraordinary fine indeed, I had bought it as a curiosity, having never seen the like; the robe was a fine Persian, or India damask; the ground white, and the flowers blue and gold, and the train held five yards; the dress under it, was a vest of the same embroider'd with gold, and set with some pearl in the work, and some turquois stones; to the vest, was a girdle five or six inches wide, after the Turkish mode; and on both ends where it join'd, or hook'd, was set with diamonds for eight inches either way, only they were not true diamonds; but no-body knew that but myself. The turban, or head-dress, had a pinacle on the top, but not about five inches, with a piece of loose sarcenet hanging from it; and on the front, just over the forehead, was a good jewel, which I had added to it. (215)

After chatting and dancing with one of the masked guests (obviously the king), Roxana stages her entrance into her drawing room:

the company presently understood that I would give them a dance by myself . . . the musick did not at first hit the tune that I directed, which was a French tune, so I was forc'd to send my woman to 'em again, standing all this while at my drawing-room door; but as soon as my woman spoke to them again, they play'd it right; and I, to let them see it was so, stepp'd forward to the middle of the room; then they began it again, and I danc'd by myself a figure which I learnt in France, when the Prince de ————

desir'd I wou'd dance for his diversion; it was indeed a very fine figure, invented by a famous master at Paris, for a lady or a gentleman to dance single; but being perfectly new, it pleas'd the company exceedingly, and they all thought it had been Turkish; nay, one gentleman had the folly to expose himself so much, as to say, and I think swore too, that he had seen it danc'd at Constantinople; which was ridiculous enough. At the finishing the dance, the company clapp'd, and almost shouted; and one of the gentlemen cry'd out, Roxana! Roxana! by ———, with an oath; upon which foolish accident I had the name of Roxana presently fix'd upon me all over the court end of town, as effectually as if I had been christen'd Roxana: I had, it seems, the felicity of pleasing every-body that night, to an extreme; and my ball, but especially my dress, was the chat of the town for that week, and so the name Roxana was the toast at, and about the court; no other health was to be nam'd with it. (216–17)[14]

The following week, Roxana gives another ball, even more splendid, attended by two beautiful ladies of quality dressed in authentic costumes from Armenia and Georgia. Rivals to Roxana, they "danc'd such a dance, as indeed, no-body there had ever seen. . . . They danc'd three times all-alone, for no-body indeed, cou'd dance with them: The novelty pleas'd, truly, but yet there was something wild and bizarre in it, because they really acted to the life the barbarous country whence they came; but as mine had the French behaviour under the Mahometan dress, it was every way as new, and pleas'd much better, indeed" (220–21).

All this cuts two ways. On the one hand, the fashion-magazine elaboration of female dress and appearance is a sign of Roxana's self-centered, empty vanity. The world she boasts of conquering is merely a collection of aristocratic drones, a lascivious court and an idle king. From one point of view, these scenes are the center of Defoe's satire, which looks disapprovingly at the immoral carnival of Restoration masquerades and thereby condemns their renewed popularity in Georgian London. But the sequence in several ways blunts the force of that satire. Roxana herself is aware to some extent of the superficiality of this world; hence, her satisfaction at fooling it so completely. Moreover, there is an implicit power in Roxana's detailed circumstantiality. Her grasp is not simply of fashion and the latest dances but of the powerful manipulation of such modes for self-expression and expansion. Defoe himself disapproved of luxuriously frivolous living such as Roxana evokes in this sequence, but the elaborate rendition of her tactics betrays his fascination with strategic brilliance as such. An impersonator himself, both as a writer of fictions and as a journalist and political operative, Defoe over and over communicates the sheer pleasure of controlling others. Roxana's emphasis lies precisely on the subtle modification of the real, its adaptation to achieve her ends. Roxana dwells on the calculated effects of her dress and dance, each not quite authentic but surpassing the real thing in its power to impress. Her "Turkish" dance is in fact French, and her authentically Turkish dress becomes an adapted artificial costume designed to draw attention. Roxana's own person is absorbed by these purposes. Thus, she boasts that she wore neither mask nor cosmetics; a crucial part of her strategy is to appear completely natural even as she manipulates nature for specific effects: "I had no mask, neither did I paint; and yet I had the day of all the ladies that appear'd at the ball, I mean of those that appear'd with faces on . . . it must be confess'd, that the habit was infinitely advantageous to me, and every-body look'd at me with a kind of pleasure" (221).

As satire or involving fantasy of sex and power, the scene is one of Defoe's most brilliant. And yet in the long run the episode becomes more than just the usual fragment of a life Defoe is so good at rendering. Superficially, the scene looks back to Roxana's giddy youth, when she "danc'd, as some say, naturally, lov'd it extremely, and sung well also" (39). But its real importance emerges only near the end of the story when it turns out to be something more than the great triumph of Roxana's life and in the process is revealed as the beginning of her increasing self-doubt and moral anguish. Roxana herself relates how her life as a courtesan began to pall, how she began to think about her past, her desertion of her children especially gnawing at her. She recounts how, through Amy's clever arrangements, she made provision for the future of her children, now adults. The two boys are set up as merchants, the two girls established financially so that they can marry well. Amy is also sent to Europe to gather news of Roxana's former lovers, the German prince and the Dutch merchant. But the latter appears in London, encountered by Roxana entirely by chance as she rides in a coach toward the city. When Amy brings news that the prince has repented his past life after nearly dying as a result of a hunting accident, Roxana agrees finally to marry the Dutch merchant.

Two opposing movements are taking place. Roxana attempts to break completely with her recent past as she disguises herself as a Quaker and leaves the fashionable world. But she also makes great efforts to reshape that past, only to realize even as she marries the merchant that the past will forever affect her present. "Thus I put an end to all the

intrieguing part of my life; a life full of prosperous wickedness; the
reflections upon which, were so much the more afflicting, as the time
had been spent in the grossest crimes, which the more I look'd back
upon, the more black and horrid they appear'd, effectually drinking up
all the comfort and satisfaction which I might otherwise have taken in
that part of life which was still before me" (287).

This sense of the past as an encircling net or inescapable weight on
the present dominates Roxana's narrative of the last phase of her life,
which is punctuated with outbursts of vivid remorse. In spite of affluence
and titles (a Dutch princess and an English baronet's lady by her
marriage to the merchant), Roxana grows "sad, heavy, pensive, and
melancholy; slept little, and eat little; dream'd continually of the most
frightful and terrible things imaginable: Nothing but apparitions of
devils and monsters, falling into gulphs, and off from steep and high
precipices, and the like" (310). But such summaries may strike a reader
as pretty predictable, merely the rhetoric of despair rather than its
substance. A much more effective rendering of guilty destiny comes at
last through the appearance of one of Roxana's daughters, Susan (named,
incidentally, after Roxana, whose real name the reader finally learns).
As it turns out, this Susan was a maid at Roxana's house in Pall Mall
where she danced to earn her name. Susan now becomes convinced
that Roxana is her mother and obsessed with finding her. Just as
Roxana is visiting a ship in the harbor that will take her and her
husband to Rotterdam, she encounters Susan, as fate would have it a
friend of the captain's wife. Such coincidences are crude enough (like
Roxana earlier finding her Dutch merchant on the road to London) as
narrative devices, but they point to Defoe's attempt to make the jump
from episodic fiction to plotted novel.

Less crude, however, is the depiction of two excruciating scenes in
which Roxana suffers in silence as she hides from the child she abandoned
so long ago, torn between guilty love and murderous rage, terrified that
Susan will reveal her scandalous past life as courtesan. Roxana's evocation
of her emotional torture ranks among Defoe's most powerful narrative
moments: "I cannot but take notice here, that notwithstanding there
was a secret horror upon my mind, and I was ready to sink when I
came close to her, to salute her; yet it was a secret inconceivable pleasure
to me when I kiss'd her, to know that I kiss'd my own child. . . .
No pen can describe, no words can express, I say, the strange impression
which this thing made upon my spirits . . . when my lips touch'd her
face; I thought I must have taken her in my arms, and kiss'd her

again a thousand times, whether I wou'd or no" (323). A few days later, Susan comes to visit Roxana. The girl's suspicions and Roxana's tangle of conflicting emotions emerge again in a scene that ties the novel's events and themes together in masterly fashion.

I was in a kind of dishabille when they came, having on a loose robe, like a morning-gown, but much after the Italian way; and I had not alter'd it when I went up, only dress'd my head a little; and as I had been represented as having been lately very ill, so the dress was becoming enough for a chamber. This morning-vest or robe, call it as you please, was more shap'd to the body, than we wear them since, showing the body in its true shape, and perhaps, a little too plainly, if it had been to be worn where any men were to come; but among ourselves it was well enough, especially for hot weather; the colour was green, figur'd; and the stuff a French damask, very rich. (330)

Susan and the captain's wife admire Roxana's dress and that leads to another vividly rendered moment from the past: "This gown, or vest, put the girl's tongue a-running again. . . . This is just such a thing as I told you, says she, the Lady danc'd in: What, says the Captain's wife, the Lady Roxana that you told me of? O! that's a charming story, says she; tell it my Lady" (331) What follows is a reprise from Susan's point of view of those crucial scenes in Roxana's life. Even as she listens "in a kind of silent rage" (331), Roxana is taken with this rehearsal of her triumphs: "I cannot help confessing what a reserve of pride still was left in me; and tho' I dreaded the sequel of the story, yet when she talk'd how handsome and how fine a lady this Roxana was, I cou'd not help being pleas'd and tickl'd with it" (334). But the climax of Susan's recollections is the Turkish dance and dress, which "she went on to describe . . . as I have done already; but did it so exactly, that I was surpriz'd at the manner of her telling it; there was not a circumstance of it left out" (335).

Susan's recollections confirm Roxana's account of her triumph; they certify the lasting effects on at least one observer of her self-dramatization. Yet the past recaptured appears in a different light, no longer simply the trajectory of Roxana's brilliant ascent up from poverty and despair to wealth and power but now revealed as part of an encircling, fateful pattern. Susan's version revises the past we thought was settled; her presence at the house in Pall Mall links Roxana's dance to her guilty past and even guiltier future. Roxana thought she was inventing herself

and breaking free, but she was in fact acting out a tragic destiny. All
this is delicately done. Roxana, as the scene begins, is fashionably precise,
luxuriously exact even as she trembles at the edge of disaster. And that
dress or "morning-vest . . . showing the body in its true shape" does
just that, reminding Susan of Roxana's Turkish dress. Fate is expressed
in character; what appear at first to be freely chosen and self-expressive
acts become part of tragic destiny. Roxana's carefully acquired poise
and sophistication turn out to be nothing less than the instruments of
her destruction.

Defoe's formal innovation in this last scene in *Roxana* is underlined
by noticing, as Michael M. Boardman does, two of its unique features.
First, it is the longest single stretch of narration in all Defoe's fiction,
and second, it represents a shift from the normal chronology of the
story.[15] Roxana inserts it as a long afterthought, telling it from what
is on the surface her happy ending as the wife of the Dutch merchant
in Holland. As she presents it, this is a confession and an explanation
of what seems at first glance excessive guilt. "I went about loaded with
crime, and altogether in the dark, as to what I was to do" (311).
What we learn at the very end of the sequence, in suitably confused
and murky fashion, is that Amy has had Susan killed, both serving
and torturing Roxana: "As for the poor girl herself, she was ever before
my eyes; I saw her by-night, and by-day; she haunted my imagination,
if she did not haunt the house; my fancy show'd her in a hundred
shapes and postures; sleeping or waking, she was with me: Sometimes
I thought I saw her with her throat cut; sometimes with her head cut,
and her brains knock'd-out; other-times hang'd upon a beam; another
time drown'd in the Great Pond at Camberwell" (374).

As Boardman says very well, "the episodic, pseudofactual mode" of
Roxana and indeed of Defoe's other narratives is exchanged here for
something radically different as the heroine changes from a "personage"
into a character and the string of events takes on "the working power
of a plot."[16] Moreover, the center of the narrative shifts from the
controlled external world of financial and sexual relationships, from
clothes, rich furniture, investments and titles, to the controlling internal
world of memory and guilt. Roxana's tortured subjectivity becomes far
more real or at least more pressing than that objective world she seemed
to have mastered, and Defoe's realism takes its most convincing psychological turn, anticipating later achievements in English and European
fiction.

Chapter Seven

Factual Narrative: A *Journal of the Plague Year*, A *Tour thro' the Whole Island of Great Britain*

Mixed in with Defoe's novels, and in some ways remarkably similar to them, are narratives we now think of as too firmly based in fact to be regarded as part of his fiction. Many of these works are enlivened by flashes of vivid reporting that make Defoe a pioneer of modern realistic journalism, and some of them also bear clear traces of his imaginative shaping. Both vivid reporting and narrative arrangement contribute to the effectiveness of Defoe's best-known piece of journalism, *A True Relation of the Apparition of One Mrs. Veal The Next Day After her Death To One Mrs. Bargrave at Canterbury, The 8th of September 1705*. Basically a ghost story such as people then were eager to believe in as proof of personal immortality, this pamphlet is an early example of Defoe's skill with crucial circumstances. He creates an authoritative air of verisimilitude with details of Mrs. Veal's age and health, the nature of her friendship with Mrs. Bargrave, the precise date and time of her visit to Canterbury, as James puts it, "precisely those details which lend substance to the ghostly Mrs. Veal's lack of it."[1] Like the narrators of the later fictional works, this reporter disarms his audience by speaking modestly and directly, inserting qualifications and corrections, not claiming to know everything and thereby sounding reliable. The narrator is supposed to be a justice of the peace at Maidstone in Kent, and he recounts in matter-of-fact fashion how Mrs. Bargrave in Canterbury was unexpectedly visited by her old friend, Mrs. Veal, who talked with her of death and the hereafter. Paraphrasing her speech and then rendering it as dialogue, Defoe achieves a lifelike version of an ordinary encounter between two old female friends. She looked ill, thought Mrs. Bargrave, as if she might have a fit: "and so placed herself in a chair just before her knees, to keep her from falling to the ground, if her fits should occasion it (for the elbow-chair, she thought, would keep her from falling on either side); and to divert Mrs. Veal, as she thought, she took hold of her gown-sleeve several times and commended it. Mrs. Veal told her it was a scoured silk, and newly made up." When Mrs. Bargrave learns that Mrs. Veal had died the previous day, she tells her story just as Defoe has told it to us. And that beautifully appropriate touch, the new "scoured silk" dress, just what two old friends would talk about, clinches it, as Mrs. Veal's sister cries out upon hearing it: "You have seen her indeed, for none knew but Mrs. Veal and myself that the gown was scoured."[2]

"This relation," the preface to *Mrs. Veal* begins, "is matter of fact, and attended with such circumstances as may induce any reasonable man to believe it."[3] Although they have been exaggerated by some critics, Defoe's powers of specific observation were very great. His ability to focus sharply on concrete particulars creates memorable moments in what are sometimes for modern readers prolix and prosy writings. And perhaps more to the point, his voracious appetite for multiplicity and variety gives some of his factual and pseudohistorical works an almost visionary quality. But Defoe's passion for the actual is often put to pious uses, and his circumstantiality is frequently enlisted, as in *Mrs. Veal,* to make the incredible possible. The facts and details he is so good at inserting into narrative thus look two ways, at their own significant reality as objects and phenomena and at a world of mystery, whether comprised of supernatural and inexplicable tokens of divine purpose as here, or full of events entirely natural but far beyond normal experience and expectations.

That simultaneous significance is the selling point of *The Storm: Or, A Collection of the most Remarkable Casualties and Disasters Which happen'd in the Late Dreadful Tempest, Both by Sea and Land* (1704). In his preface to this gathering of eyewitness accounts of the hurricanelike winds that had just caused great damage in England, Defoe stresses the obvious divine origin of "the dreadfulest and most universal judgment that ever almighty power thought fit to bring upon this part of the world." Winds, as he says later in the book, are essentially unexplained by philosophers and, more than other natural phenomena, "directly lead us to speculations and refer us to infinite power."[4] But as he stitches together letters describing the unparalleled destruction wrought by the tempest, Defoe evokes another kind of wonder, provoked not so much by divine power as by the natural plenitude of a world of unprecedented quantities in which he is a nearly indefatigable enumerator: "Nor shall

I often trouble the reader with the multitude or magnitude of trees blown down, whole parks ruin'd, fine walks defac'd, and orchards laid flat, and the like: and tho' I had my self the curiosity to count the number of trees, in a circuit I rode, over most part of Kent, in which being tired with the number, I left off reckoning after I had gone on to 17000; and tho' I have great reason to believe I did not observe one half of the quantity."[5]

Most of Defoe's work deals in one way or another with this divided understanding of the world. As we have seen in books like *An Essay on the History and Reality of Apparitions* (1727), he consistently tried to balance his belief in traditional religious explanations of the world with his sophisticated knowledge of modern science. In a book that bridges, in a sense, the gap between his fiction and nonfiction, *Serious Reflections During the Life . . . of Robinson Crusoe*, Defoe has Crusoe search for a moderate position whereby God's providence works both in the "silent voice . . . of his managing events and causes" and by "silent messengers on many occasions, whether sleeping or waking, whether directly or indirectly, whether by hints, impulses, allegories, mysteries, or otherwise, we know not." God still speaks, Crusoe insists, and "even his immediate voice from heaven, is not entirely ceased from us, though it may have changed the mediums of communication."[6] For Defoe the compiler of *The Storm,* the destructive winds are plainly just such a message from God. Yet for the fictional narrator of Defoe's most convincing "factual" narrative the origins and purposes of catastrophe are much less clear.

A Journal of the Plague Year (1722) reflects Defoe's concern about a possible recurrence of plague in England. Along with *Due Preparations for the Plague, as well for Soul as Body,* published the same year, this reconstruction of the months when bubonic plague ravaged London in 1665 was intended as a warning. Defoe may also have been writing to provide indirect support for the quarantine measures the government had instituted in the summer of 1721 to protect against foreign infection. The danger of such recurrence was real enough, and in *Applebee's Journal* during September and October of 1720, Defoe had written vivid accounts of the plague then raging in southern France. Scholars used to think that Defoe had worked closely from a real diary, and that the experiences of the narrator, like the statistics of death, the "bills of mortality" with which the book abounds, were drawn from documentary records. Identified at the end by the initials "H. F." the narrator is clearly modeled on Defoe's uncle, Henry Foe, then about thirty-seven. It is now clear that, as usual, Defoe transformed what he borrowed, taking over the facts and statistics available to evoke a reality he had never actually experienced and making *A Journal of the Plague Year* a work of imagination, both fact and fiction.

At first glance, *A Journal of the Plague Year* looks like religious business as usual and falls into a familiar pious pattern. As J. Paul Hunter points out, the book grew out of what he calls "the providence and diary traditions" so important to the seventeenth-century Puritan religious consciousness.[7] Like *Robinson Crusoe,* it deals with the key themes of Christian experience and its narrator attempts to translate its events into Christianity's recurring patterns, which Paul Korshin summarizes as "apostasy, threats of destruction and death, repentance, and the promise of salvation." But Defoe's narrator is not, after all, a professional sermonizer and his journal is not "a typological exegesis" that "explains the types in *another* text."[8] Instead, the narrator has no clear or certain way of explaining the plague; he is simply an anguished yet scrupulously careful observer of events, much of the time a sort of camera eye. As Defoe seems to have deliberately conceived it, *A Journal of the Plague Year* requires not a professional preacher or exegete but a bewildered individual (a bachelor with no family, a merchant worried about his business of selling saddles), attempting to apply Christian categories to what he sees in order to find their consoling patterns. The book dramatizes the difficulty of that pious effort for a thoughtful layperson in the face of an appalling natural disaster.

In other words, the book is convincingly authentic because it evokes confusion and uncertainty. It is also, undeniably, confusing and repetitive, digressive and rambling. Most critics tend to see these qualities as effectively controlled and expressive. The repetitions and recurring topics are part of Defoe's realistic plan and contribute to the book's effectiveness. Paul Alkon finds that they allow readers "to experience a duration that corresponds as clearly as the aesthetic experience of any reading-time could to the distinctive way in which moments passed and were filled by recurrent rhythms during London's plague."[9] But what sustains interest and holds the book together in spite of its lack of structure is precisely, as Everett Zimmerman puts it, "the disorienting force of the plague" rather than Defoe's structuring of the narrative. *A Journal* works best, like so much of Defoe, at the level of particular episodes, in certain vividly observed individual moments. The material world presents itself so powerfully that the narrator "cannot fully reconcile it with his religious assumptions."[10] Or to put it another way, the plague imagined in all its horrible, specifically quantified immensity, filtered through the vividly rendered experience of a fully realized individual, challenges the ordered connection between that material world and divine Providence that Defoe speaks of so confidently elsewhere.

Near the very end of his harrowing story, the saddler concludes "that *the best physic against the plague is to run away from it.*" People think, he goes on, that God will preserve them, but "this kept thousands in the town whose carcases went into the great pits by cartloads, and who, if they had fled from the danger, had, I believe, been safe from the disaster; at least 'tis probable they had been safe."[11] Why, then, against all the odds and common sense did he stay? His answer is one Defoe would have understood: circumstances prevented him each time he started to leave, and this pattern of events hinted by their concurrence at divine ordering.

It came very warmly into my mind one morning as I was musing on this particular thing, that as nothing attended us without the direction or permission of Divine Power, so these disappointments must have something in them extraordinary; and I ought to consider whether it did not evidently point out, or intimate to me, that it was the will of Heaven I should not go. It immediately followed in my thoughts, that if it really was from God that I should stay, He was able effectually to preserve me in the midst of all the death and danger that would surround me; and that if I attempted to secure myself by fleeing from my habitation, and acted contrary to these intimations, which I believe to be Divine, it was a kind of flying from God, and that he would cause His justice to overtake me when and where He thought fit. (32)

Like Crusoe, the saddler looks for God's silent messages and warns that his circumstances are entirely his own. What he describes is a method of self-scrutiny that each person must apply to his or her own case: "he should keep his eye upon the particular providences which occur at that time, and look upon them complexly, as they regard one another" (31). And yet, again like Crusoe, the saddler knows that action is necessary. "To be utterly careless of ourselves in such cases," says Crusoe, "and talk of trusting Providence is a lethargy of the worst nature; for as we are to trust Providence with our estates, and to use at the same time, all diligence in our callings; so we are to trust Providence with our safety, but with our eyes open, to all its necessary cautions, warnings, and instructions."[12] When his brother laughs at his sense of heavenly intimations, the saddler changes his mind. Here and throughout the narrative he warns against fatalism, whether the "pre-destinating notions" of the "Turks and Mahometans in Asia" (33) his brother tells him about, or closer to home the "brutal courage" of the London poor, "who ran into any business which they could get employment in, though it was the most hazardous" (106–7).

At last, the saddler convinces himself to stay by means of bibliomancy, a traditional gambit for gaining divine direction by looking at random in the Bible. By chance, he stops at the ninety-first Psalm, long thought to have been written by King David in time of plague: "I will say of the Lord, He is my refuge and my fortress: my God, in Him will I trust. Surely He shall deliver me from the snare of the fowler, and from the noisome pestilence" (34). As Everett Zimmerman points out, not only was bibliomancy treated as unreliable and arbitrary by many at the time but the saddler's reading of Psalm 91 is selective and omits the passage quoted by the devil in the New Testament when he tempts Christ: "For he shall give his angels charge over thee, to keep thee in all thy ways. They shall bear thee up in their hands, lest thou dash thy foot against a stone." Zimmerman raises a key question: "Is H. F. to be commended for his trust in God, or is he wrongfully presuming on God's mercy? The narrator's confidence in his decision cannot be the reader's ."[13]

Zimmerman assumes a skeptical modern reader or a very thoughtful, scripturally sophisticated eighteenth-century reader, both licensed by Defoe's narrative to feel morally superior to the saddler. Instead, Defoe's main object in A Journal seems to be to create sympathy rather than moral judgment. The saddler's confusion and, especially, his clumsy efforts to rationalize his decision to stay intensify that sympathy. In a very practical sense, the saddler has to stay so that Defoe can tell readers about the plague, but the vividly detailed evocation of its ghastly effects makes his decision to stay all the more irrational and difficult to defend. And yet the saddler's anguish and uncertainty even as he stays are part of the larger effect of the plague, whose ravages are psychological as well as physical, bringing moral and intellectual confusion as well as death.

Defoe has two intertwined stories or two alternating perspectives, personal and historical, from which to tell one story. The saddler is a guilty survivor and fascinated observer, rather like the rest of Defoe's heroes. Choosing to stay for no good or at least no clear reason, the saddler acts out his own freely chosen destiny, but at the same time he believes he is deferring to God's will. Just so, Defoe's protagonists

are self-made and strongly willful survivors who are also produced by
their social and historical circumstances and are, in some cases, trying
to convince themselves that their lives were all along in God's hands.
The saddler's dilemma is an intensely concentrated version of the problem
of self-determination they all face and that occupies Defoe himself to
the point of obsession. Modern and secular, activist and interventionist
in his view of nature and society, Defoe was also as we have seen a
staunch economic traditionalist, an unbending Puritan moralist and
amateur theologian. On these matters, his heroes are mostly inconsistent,
but the saddler is forced to be more thoughtful. He tries in the course
of the journal to negotiate between various kinds of explanations for
the plague, its causes and origins, its treatment or avoidance. Even in
the effects of the plague itself he finds opposing or complementary,
balancing results: death and desolation all around, but also a communal
unity and examples of individual courage and loyalty; economic disaster
and an overseas ban on goods exported from London, but when the
plague and the next year's great fire were over, "there never was known
such a trade all over England" (233). He puts his trust in God's special
Providence but is skeptical of other predictive phenomena like the comet
that appeared over the city before the plague. He knows, like Defoe,
"that natural causes are assigned by the astronomers for such things,
and that their motions and even their revolutions are calculated, or
pretended to be calculated, so that they cannot be so perfectly called
the forerunners or foretellers, much less the procurers, of such events
as pestilence, war, fire, and the like" (41). In the end, he concludes
just as Defoe himself would have that the plague had natural rather
than supernatural causes. Nonetheless, he "reflect[s] upon no man for
putting the reason of those things upon the immediate hand of God,
and the appointment and direction of His providence" (205). But, in
an odd and revealing phrase, he calls his own deliverance "one next
to miraculous" (205), and as he proceeds, explaining how God works
through "the ordinary course of natural causes," one can see rational
inference based on careful observation replacing religious explanations.

He is pleased to act by those natural causes as the ordinary means, excepting
and reserving to Himself nevertheless a power to act in a supernatural way
when He sees occasion. Now 'tis evident that in the case of an infection
there is no apparent extraordinary occasion for supernatural operation, but
the ordinary course of things appears sufficiently armed, and made capable
of all the effects that Heaven usually directs by a contaigon. Among these

causes and effects, this of the secret conveyance of infection, imperceptible and unavoidable, is more than sufficient to execute the fierceness of Divine vengeance, without putting it upon supernaturals and miracle. The acute penetrating nature of the disease itself was such, and the infection was received so imperceptibly, that the most exact caution could not secure us while in the place. But I must be allowed to believe—and I have so many examples fresh in my memory to convince me of it, that I think none can resist their evidence—I say, I must be allowed to believe that no one in this whole nation ever received the sickness or infection but who received it in the ordinary way of infection from somebody, or the clothes or touch or stench of somebody that was infected before. (205–6)

Although the book is hardly that neat, a clear awareness of natural process has replaced the saddler's initial confusion and uncertainty. He has in a sense earned his clarity by staying and observing it all up close and at first hand, the hero not as resolute man of action but as scrupulously accurate observer of whatever may happen. Watching at times from his window but also walking the streets, the saddler does not flinch from trying to render the awful things he sees and hears: "I wish I could repeat the very sound of those groans and of those exclamations that I heard from some poor dying creatures when in the height of their agonies and distress, and that I could make him that reads this hear, as I imagine I now hear them, for the sound seems still to ring in my ears" (120).

And yet for all the unforgettable horrors of the city streets, littered with corpses, echoing with the screams of the dying, the saddler finds himself driven by "unsatisfied curiosity" through "many dismal scenes . . . as particularly of persons falling dead in the streets, terrible shrieks and screechings of women, who, in their agonies, would throw open their chamber windows and cry out in a dismal, surprising manner. It is impossible to describe the variety of postures in which the passions of the poor people would express themselves" (98). The infinite variety of human and natural possibility is Defoe's great theme in his factual works, and the saddler's compulsive curiosity renders the plague as a fascinating plenitude of horror. The high point of that fullness is the saddler's visit to the "great pit in the churchyard of our parish of Aldgate" (77).

As people begin to die in droves, ordinary graves hardly suffice, so mass burials are arranged in pits that are made progressively larger. The saddler spares us no details, noting that because of the danger of infection the magistrates order that graves must be at least six feet deep. Horror thrives, in *A Journal,* on exactitude; the saddler's estimates are precise: "As near as I may judge, it was about forty feet in length, and about fifteen or sixteen feet broad, and at the time I first looked at it, about nine feet deep; but it was said they dug it near twenty feet deep afterwards" (77–78). As the pit is enlarged and the bodies piled up in it, the saddler admits that "curiosity led, or rather drove, me to go and see this pit again, when there had been near 400 people buried in it" (79). Moreover, as he notes with alarming candor, he was not content to see it in the day time as he had before. For then the bodies were covered with loose earth. "I resolved to go in the night and see some of them thrown in" (79). The saddler hesitates, warned by the sexton, who tells him the sight is shocking beyond words. A cart arrives with sixteen or seventeen bodies, and the saddler's account of their tumbling into the pit is curiously unsentimental: "some were wrapt up in linen sheets, some in rags, some little other than naked, or so loose that what covering they had fell from them in the shooting out of the cart, and they fell quite naked among the rest" (81). In addition, the saddler also sees another observer, a man he discovers whose wife and several children are among the dead in the cart. As this man watches the bodies "shot into the pit promiscuously" (80), he faints with grief and shock, so that he has to be carried to a nearby tavern. "This," says the saddler, "was a mournful scene indeed, and affected me almost as much as the rest" (81).

This grieving man underlines the saddler's peculiar and privileged status in the plague. Although hardly dispassionate, the saddler is at a safe distance from its disabling effects, somehow immune so that he can enumerate these staggering statistics and gaze without wavering into the great pit, noting the dispositions of the bodies and dramatizing the inarticulate, fainting grief of others. For all his local confusions and repetitions, the saddler in the end delivers a coherent account and, perhaps more important, one that makes the jump from anguished personal journal to clear-sighted historical rendering of these events.

Indeed, from the first the saddler tells us a great deal about the larger social and political world, and his journal is always much more than a subjective account of what he saw and felt. Not only does he reproduce the grim bills of mortality and the measures the city magistrates imposed to control the plague, but he gives us a sense of London itself as a physical and historical entity. Thus, he walks specific streets and neighborhoods, noting the progress of the disease parish by parish, the

closing of the food markets so that the country people sold their
provisions "in the fields beyond Whitechapel, in Spittlefields; also in
St. George's Fields in Southwark, in Bunhill Fields, and in a great
field called Wood's Close, near Islington" (97). The City of London
itself, the old central commercial district where the saddler lives, is now
deserted, its streets more like green fields than busy thoroughfares: "the
great streets within the city, such as Leadenhall Street, Bishopsgate
Street, Cornhill, and even the Exchange itself, had grass growing in
them in several places; neither cart or coach were seen in the streets
from morning to evening" (117).

A large part of his description of London is evocative, growing out
of his subjective response: "London might well be said to be all in
tears: the mourners did not go about the streets indeed, for nobody
put on black or made a formal dress of mourning for their nearest
friends; but the voice of mourners was truly heard in the streets. The
shrieks of women and children at the windows and doors of their
houses . . . were so frequent to be heard as we passed the streets,
that it was enough to pierce the stoutest heart in the world to hear
them" (37). But the saddler grounds his vivid personal impressions in
social and political facts. Thanks to specific historical developments,
London is full of people: "the wars being over, the armies disbanded,
and the royal family and the monarchy being restored," great numbers
"had flocked to London to settle in business, or to depend upon and
attend the Court for rewards of services, preferments, and the like"
(39). The saddler notes that many blamed the court's "crying vices"
for bringing this terrible judgment on the nation, but chiefly he merely
records the socioeconomic situation caused by the Restoration: "As this
conflux of the people to a youthful and gay Court made a great trade
in the city, especially in everything that belonged to fashion and finery,
so it drew by consequence a great number of workmen, manufacturers,
and the like, being mostly poor people who depended upon their labour"
(39–40).

Although the plague is no respecter of rank, as the economic situation
is disrupted the poor suffer more than other groups, even though the
magistrates do much to alleviate their suffering and, not incidentally,
to prevent insurrection. "Let any one who is acquainted with what
multitudes of people get their daily bread in this city by their labour,
whether artificers or mere workmen—I say, let any man consider what
must be the miserable condition of this town if, on a sudden, they
should be all turned out of employment, that labour should cease, and

wages for work be no more" (113). London's nightmare, for the saddler and for Defoe, is socioeconomic as much as it is biological. There are individual poor people who behave heroically, like the waterman at Blackwell who moves the saddler to tears by his selfless devotion to his family, and the three men from Wapping, the biscuit maker, carpenter, and sailmaker who retreat to the countryside and bravely survive there by their wits. As a group, however, the poor are an enormous, threatening unruly mass, driven by "the usual impetuosity of their tempers, full of outcries and lamentations when taken, but madly careless of themselves, foolhardy and obstinate, while they were well" (220). So they die "by heaps" (220). The saddler also records the unprecedented charity the now boundless misery of the poor provokes, as much as a hundred thousand pounds a week distributed by the local authorities over and above the private charity of individuals. With his comprehensive view of these staggering numbers, the saddler strikes a balance. The historical record he sets straight tends to compensate for the confused enormity of the plague year.

A Journal of the Plague Year, then, is as much historical analysis as it is a testament of personal experience. The saddler looks out from and beyond his own subjectivity, which is inseparable as he recounts it from the history of his times. As one critic suggests, the real hero of the book is London itself, and *A Journal* is "testimony of a city's victory in the face of a disaster of frightful proportion."[14] As he considers his experiences, the saddler's views become panoramic, informed by a sophisticated awareness of the larger historical consequences of the plague. But Defoe, as Maximillian E. Novak puts it, was "a propagandist and a journalist more than he was a historian."[15] Although he wrote a number of books that are histories in the sense that they are reasonably objective and comprehensive, Defoe's best historical writing is journalistic in that it derives its effectiveness from a subjective observer. Like journalism, it delivers what history feels like a day at a time. *A Journal of the Plague Year* balances the enormous and often unwieldy extent of history against the daily experience of an individual who has lived through it.

In this sense, the book has much in common with Defoe's other pseudohistorical narratives, especially *Memoirs of a Cavalier* (1720), a narrative of the Thirty Years War and the English Civil War in the middle of the seventeenth century. That story is told by someone who fought on the losing side in the civil war, a Cavalier, as the supporters of the royalist cause were called, and his forthright, soldierly manner makes him very different from the earnest saddler. But the Cavalier like the saddler brings back a vividly individualized report of great and consequential historical events. Several of these, like the plague at its most horrific, both defy description and testify to Defoe's fascination with disaster, whether natural or man-made. In search of military glory, the young Cavalier joins the army of the Catholic Austrian emperor under Count Tilly as it lays siege to the German Protestant city of Magdeburgh. He arrives to witness the taking of the city and the slaughter of its inhabitants: "This calamity sure was the dreadfullest sight that ever I saw; the rage of the imperial soldiers was most intolerable, and not to be expressed; of 25000, some said 30000 people, there was not a soul to be seen alive, till the flames drove those that were hid in vaults and secret places to seek death in the streets, rather than perish in the fire."[16] Like the saddler, the Cavalier provides close-up views within a historical panorama: "we could see the poor people in crowds driven down the streets, flying from the fury of the soldiers who followed butchering them as fast as they could, and refused mercy to any body; 'till driving them to the river's edge, the desperate wretches would throw themselves into the river, where thousands of them perished, especially women and children" (45).

Memoirs of a Cavalier is not often this bloody, although it does show the hero growing disillusioned with the royalist cause and sick of killing his own countrymen. What gives it Defoe's stamp is the special quality of its hero, an observer of his own private reactions as well as a recorder of public events. "I found a strange secret and unaccountable sadness upon my spirits to see this acting in my own native country. It grieved me to the heart, even in the rout of our enemies, to see the slaughter of them; and even in the fight, to hear a man cry for quarter in English moved me to a compassion which I had never been used to" (165). In a modest way, the book is like a novel, for its hero comes to a changed self-consciousness and in the final pages the reader is told more about his adventurous escape from the victorious parliamentary forces than about the resolution of the war. That balance between private and public, sometimes tipped toward the former, is a persistent feature of Defoe's view of history.

But however vivid and convincing these pseudohistorical works are, they are still triumphs of imagination, dealing with events that happened before Defoe was born, reconstructed from documents by the man one critic long ago called "a great, a truly great liar, perhaps the greatest liar that ever lived."[17] But one of Defoe's works is solidly based on actual experience, indeed on the accumulated experience of most of his life. *A Tour thro' the Whole Island of Great Britain* was published in three separate volumes from 1724 to 1726, and in the preface to the first volume Defoe underlines the currency of his account: "The situation of things is given not as they have been, but as they are; the improvements in the soil, the product of the earth, the labour of the poor, the improvement in manufactures, in merchandizes, in navigation, all respects the present time, not the time past."[18] Even in *A Journal of the Plague Year* and *Memoirs of a Cavalier,* Defoe was really more interested in the present than the past he seemed to specialize in recreating. *A Journal* is a warning that plague may come again. The saddler's celebration of the religious unity created by the plague is an implicit commentary on the dangers of religious divisions in the England of 1722, as is the Cavalier's descriptions of the fratricidal civil war of the 1640s. But the present as Defoe defines it in *A Tour* is a dynamic entity, changing every day, so that his book is both accurate and obsolete: "for the face of things so often alters, and the situation of affairs in this great British Empire gives such new turns, even to nature it self, that there is matter of new observation every day presented to the traveller's eye" (1:2). As he opens the second volume, Defoe repeats this theme, giving it even more emphasis, celebrating England as a nation committed to transforming itself continually: "New foundations are always laying, new buildings always raising, highways repairing, churches and public buildings erecting, fires and other calamities happening, fortunes of families taking different turns, new trades are every day erected, new projects enterpriz'd, new designs laid; so that as long as England is a trading, improving nation, no perfect description either of the place, the people, or the conditions and state of things can be given" (1:252).

A Tour is a comprehensive guide to Great Britain, based in large part on Defoe's trips over the years through just about every one of its counties and major cities. To some extent, it is also based on other books, although Defoe never admits this. His chief rival and predecessor was John Macky, whose *Journey through England* appeared in two volumes, one in 1714, the other in 1722. One historian estimates that Defoe cribbed about one-tenth of the whole from various authorities. Like *A Journal of the Plague Year,* it turns out, *A Tour* is a fabrication. Or, more accurately, the book is a composite of Defoe's reading and his experiences of the previous fifty years.[19] *A Tour* examines Britain's counties and cities, their economy, geography, and social and political structures. But it has a concrete and specific base in personal experience.

Defoe visits the people, tours the stately homes and gardens of the wealthy and powerful, interviews miners and peasants, merchants and fishermen. Most of all, he observes in person and on the spot the actual flow of trade and commerce and marvels at the volume of goods whose circulation he evokes. As Defoe describes the movement of produce and manufactured goods to London, his imagination is stirred by the immensity of it all. Over and over he is struck by the "prodigious quantities" of goods and people, by Britain's inexhaustible fertility. As so often in his writing, Defoe is drawn to celebrate plenitude and tirelessly sings the wonder of quantities beyond individual comprehension: the million and a half turkeys driven to London from Suffolk each year, the uncountable number of mackerel caught off the Dorsetshire coast, the hundreds of thousands of sheep sold at the Weyhill fair in Wiltshire, the corn markets at London ("the whole world cannot equal the quantity bought and sold here" [1:345]), and the seemingly endless lines of ships in the river from London Bridge to Blackwall: "The thing is a kind of infinite, and the parts to be separated from one another in such a description, are so many, that it is hard to know where to begin" (1:347).

But Defoe also enumerates with unflagging curiosity individual parts of this huge canvas, the gear and tackle of trades, whole bills of lading and inventories of barns and warehouses. He is especially fascinated by the way things work, by symmetries and systems in nature and in human artifice, and sometimes in wonderful combinations of the two. Thus, in Yorkshire he describes the way the clothing manufacture cooperates with the landscape. The houses of the clothiers are built upon the sides of the coal-rich hills so that they can use the downward running streams and burn the coal to process their textiles: "as the drying-houses, scouring-shops and places where they used this water, emitted the water again, ting'd with the drugs of the dying fat, and with the oil, the soap, the tallow, and other ingredients used by the clothiers in dressing and scouring, etc. which then runs away thro' the lands to the next, the grounds are not only universally watered, how dry soever the season, but that water so ting'd and so fatten'd enriches the lands they run through, that 'tis hardly to be imagined how fertile and rich the soil is made by it" (2:194–95). With similar satisfaction, Defoe traces the circular system in the fertility of the downs (hills) and valleys around Dorchester: "The grass, or herbage of these downs is full of the sweetest, and the most aromatick plants, such as nourish the sheep to a strange degree, and the sheeps dung again nourishes that herbage to a strange degree; so that the valleys are render'd extreamly fruitful, by the washing of the water in hasty showers from off these hills" (1:211). Defoe also appreciates purely human constructions, providing expertly detailed architectural appreciations of St. Paul's Cathedral and Windsor Castle. Pursuing a favorite theme and recurring discovery, Defoe describes in detail the composition of Roman roads he has seen dug up: "I have observ'd flint-stones, chalk-stones, hard gravel, solid hard clay, and several other sorts of earth laid in layers, like the veins of oar in a mine; a laying of clay of a solid binding quality, then flint-stones, then chalk, then upon the chalk rough ballast or gravel, 'till the whole work has been rais'd six or eight foot from the bottom; then it has been cover'd with a crown or rising ridge in the middle, gently sloping to the sides, that the rain might run off every way, and not soak into the work" (2:119).

As those superior Roman roads hint, *A Tour* is also a moral, and sometimes an eloquently elegiacal work, marking not only progress and prosperity but decline and fall, the inevitable waxing and waning that is "the fate of things, by which we see that towns, kings, countries, families, and persons, have all their elevation, their medium, their declination, and even their destruction in the womb of time, and the course of nature" (1:54). At times, *A Tour* is unabashedly chauvinistic, a sort of chamber of commerce brochure about the greatness of England. Just outside London, for example, Defoe visits Cannons, the extravagantly opulent palace built by the Duke of Chandos. In Italy such houses belong to "sovereign princes, or have been ages in their building" (2:7), but Cannons was built in three years, and the duke (a relative parvenu, by the way, James Brydges, who had made his fortune by serving as paymaster general from 1707 to 1712) lives in a grandeur and magnificence that no nobleman in England can equal. In the same vein, Defoe traces with satisfaction the emergence of new fortunes, pointing to the elegant suburban retreats of fabulously wealthy merchants in the Surrey countryside near London, compiling a list of rising families "of citizens and tradesmen" who before long "will equal the families of the ancient gentry" (1:15). But there is a darker side to progress and the march of new money. The sunny vision of England clouds over from time to time: "It would also take up a large chapter in this book, to but mention the overthrow, and catastrophe of innumerable wealthy city families, who after they have thought their houses establish'd, and have built their magnificent country seats, as well as others, have

sunk under the misfortunes of business, and the disasters of trade, after
the world has thought them pass'd all possibility of danger" (1:169).

As Defoe himself admitted, he was not a systematic writer. "I must
beg the reader's indulgence," he says in *Augusta Triumphans* (1728),
"being the most unmethodical writer imaginable; 'tis true, I lay down
a scheme, but fancy is so fertile I often start fresh hints, and cannot
but pursue them."[20] So *A Tour* is an enormous improvisation given
superficial coherence by the geographical boundaries of Britain and
something of a plot by the economic contrast between the cultivated
South and the increasingly barren and undeveloped face of things Defoe
encounters as he travels northward. But thanks to Defoe's energetic
honesty, he finds himself drawn into a recurring set of contrasts and
paradoxes that create a unifying balance as they weigh against his
normal enthusiasm. In the middle of prosperity in Somersetshire, Defoe
is surrounded by beggars, who swell to a crowd after he throws them
some coins, "as if the whole town was come out into the street, and
they ran in this manner after us through the whole street, and a great
way after we were quite out of the town" (1:265). Even as he marvels
at the swelling development of London, he predicts that the stock
market will in time collapse when the public debt on which it is
founded is paid and the "overgrown city" will shrink as "the vast
concourse of people . . . will separate again and disperse as naturally
as they have now crouded hither: What will be the fate then of all
the fine buildings in the out parts, in such a case, let any one judge"
(1:337). Turned cheerfully to the expanding future and deliberately set
against rehashing the past, Defoe promises over and over again to leave
it to the antiquarians: "Matters of antiquity are not my enquiry, but
principally observations on the present state of things" (1:69). Old
mythologies are banished in favor of present realities, which are in any
case more beautiful to contemplate: "I shall talk nothing of the marriage
of old Isis, the male river, with the beautiful Thame, the female river,
a whimsy as simple as the subject was empty, but I shall speak of the
river as occasion presents, as it really is made glorious by the splendor
of its shores . . . with the greatest bridge, and the greatest city in the
world" (1:173). Nonetheless, he is drawn to the past, sometimes only
to ridicule local legends and persistent ancient superstitions, but sometimes
because it is attractive, eloquent in its remains and able to provoke
eloquence in Defoe himself. After traveling through the three northwest
counties of Lancashire, Westmoreland, and Cumberland, Defoe repents
his early resolve "to decline the delightful view of antiquity, here being

so great and so surprizing a variety, and every day more and more discovered." Such remains, he finds, "are beautiful, even in their decay, and the venerable face of antiquity has some thing so pleasing, so surprizing, so satisfactory in it . . . that I know nothing renders travelling more pleasant and more agreeable" (2:254).

The past is attractive in other ways. For example, those Roman roads Defoe described with such admiration could not now be built: "labour is dear, wages high, no man works for bread and water now; our labourers do not work in the road, and drink in the brook; so that as rich as we are, it would exhaust the whole nation to build the edifices, the causways, the aqueducts, lines, castles, fortifications, and other publick works, which the Romans built with very little expense" (2:120). And yet in spite of this pampered modern labor force, Defoe encounters in Derbyshire lead miners whose lives are as miserable as Roman slaves, who work in shafts up to 150 yards under the ground, whose families live in caves, and who earn no more than eight pence a day. One of these miners rises out of his shaft like an apparition, and Defoe's account is balanced between pity and surprise: "he was as lean as a skeleton, pale as a dead corps, his hair and beard a deep black, his flesh lank, and, as we thought, something of the colour of the lead itself, [we] fancied he look'd like an inhabitant of the dark regions below" (2:164). The scene is both curious and moving, yet another rarity in his travelogue but also a moral lesson "for the discontented part of the rich world how to value their own happiness, by looking below them, and seeing how others live" (2:160).

All in all, Defoe's *Tour* is a richly varied work, more unified, less didactic than any of his other factual works, informed by a controlled moral irony missing from his fiction. In a sense, it is Defoe's most artistic piece of work, displaying what Pat Rogers calls a "marked awareness of formal design." Rogers points to the construction of the book around a series of trips to and from London, so that the picture we have in the end is of the "process of human geography" whereby London is the center and heart of the nation.[21] A compendium of Defoe's interests and attitudes, *A Tour* also provides, partly because of its length and variety, a uniquely clarifying context for them. Insofar as is possible, Defoe appears here in his own person rather than as an assumed personality. Freed to a large extent from the pressures of impersonation and from the constraints of a narrow didactic purpose, Defoe sometimes achieves a new relationship to the actual. Instead of selecting and arranging facts to prove a point or illustrate a thesis,

Defoe often eloquently defers to the material world, noting its resistance to interpretation and confessing his inability to do more than observe. These moments crop up especially in the bleak stretches of the northern counties, such as Lancashire and Westmoreland, "a country eminent only for being the wildest, most barren and frightful of any that I have passed over in England" (2:269–70). But that wildness is relieved by the sight of "some very pleasant, populous and manufacturing towns" to which he turns with relief, since " 'tis of no advantage to represent horror" (2:270). At other moments, horror at useless nature is not the issue. Here is his brilliant sketch of the fen country in Lincolnshire:

This part is indeed very properly call'd Holland, for 'tis a flat, level, and often drowned country, like Holland itself; here the very ditches are navigable, and the people pass from town to town in boats, as in Holland: Here we had the uncouth musick of the bittern, a bird formerly counted ominous and presaging, and who, as fame tells us, (but I believe no body knows) throws its bill into a reed, and then gives the dull, heavy groan or sound, like a sigh, which it does so loud, that with a deep base, like the sound of a gun at a great distance, 'tis heard two or three miles, (say the people) but perhaps not quite so far. (2:95)

Defoe records isolated phenomena with a detached accuracy and disinterested honesty that makes them more oddly convincing, more finally real than any of the social and economic panorama of *A Tour*. Moments like this establish, as much as anything in his fiction, Defoe's status as a great innovator of realistic narrative.

Notes and References

Chapter One

1. *The Compleat English Gentleman*, ed. Karl D. Bulbring (London: David Nutt, 1890), 218–20. I have modernized quotations from Defoe's correspondence but retained original spelling and punctuation in all quotations from his published works. I have eliminated most of the italics and capitalized common nouns that were a feature of eighteenth-century printing and, normally, had no particular authorial significance.

2. *The Present State of the Parties in Great Britain* (1712), 295–96. Cited in John Robert Moore, *Daniel Defoe: Citizen of the Modern World* (Chicago: University of Chicago Press, 1958), 33.

3. *Compleat English Gentleman*, 200–201.

4. *Review*, 22 October 1709, in *Defoe's Review*, ed. Arthur Wellesley Secord, 22 vols. (New York: Columbia University Press, 1938), 6:341. This is a facsimile edition. On Defoe's intellectual arrogance as a young man, see F. Bastian, *Defoe's Early Life* (Totowa, N. J.: Barnes & Noble, 1981), 64–65.

5. Bastian, *Defoe's Early Life*, 122.

6. Moore, *Daniel Defoe*, 85.

7. *A Tour through the Whole Island of Great Britain*, 2 vols. (London: J. M. Dent & Sons, 1962), 1:298.

8. John Oldmixon, *The History of England, During the Reign of King William and Queen Mary* (1735), 37. Cited in Moore, *Daniel Defoe*, 71.

9. James Sutherland, *Defoe* (London: Methuen, 1937), 50.

10. Letter of May-June 1704, in *The Letters of Daniel Defoe*, ed. George Harris Healey (Oxford: Clarendon Press, 1955), 17.

11. *An Appeal to Honour and Justice* (1715), in *The Novels and Selected Writings of Daniel Defoe*, 14 vols. (Oxford: Blackwell's, 1927–28), 13:195.

12. *The True-Born Englishman*, in *Selected Poetry and Prose of Daniel Defoe*, ed. Michael F. Shugrue (New York: Holt, Rinehart & Winston, 1968), 49.

13. Frank Ellis, Introduction to *Poems on Affairs of State: Augustan Satirical Verse, 1660–1714* (New Haven: Yale University Press, 1970), xxxii. Ellis remarks that Defoe is the dominant satirical poet of these years (xxxi).

14. *The History of the Kentish Petition*, in *Novels and Selected Writings*, 13:91, 112.

15. Moore, *Daniel Defoe*, 108.

16. *The Shortest Way with the Dissenters*, in *Selected Poetry and Prose*, ed. Shugrue, 116.

17. Sutherland, *Defoe*, 89.

18. Letter of 9 January 1703, in *Letters of Defoe,* ed. Healey, 1–2.

19. *Appeal to Honour and Justice,* in *Novels and Selected Writings,* 13:199.

20. "A Hymn to the Pillory," in *Novels and Selected Writings,* 13:137, 151.

21. Bastian, *Defoe's Early Life,* 300.

22. Letter of April 1703, in *Letters of Defoe,* ed. Healey, 4.

23. Letter of July–August 1704, in ibid., 31.

24. Ibid., 43. See Sutherland, *Defoe,* 149.

25. *Review,* 9 January 1706, in *Defoe's Review,* 3:639.

26. Sutherland, *Defoe,* 106.

27. Ibid., 180–81. See the *Review,* 2 November 1710, in *Defoe's Review,* 7:377.

28. *Review,* 26 June 1712, in ibid., 8:790.

29. *Appeal to Honour and Justice,* in *Novels and Selected Writings,* 13:238.

30. *Mist's Weekly Journal,* 20 September 1718, in William Lee, *Daniel Defoe: His Life, and Recently Discovered Writings,* 3 vols. (London: Hotten, 1869), 2:71.

31. *Appeal to Honour and Justice,* in *Novels and Selected Writings,* 13:229.

32. John Robert Moore, *A Checklist of The Writings of Daniel Defoe,* 2d ed. (1960; reprint ed., Hamden, Conn.: Archon Books, 1971), 1.

33. "Preface," in *Review* (London, 1712), n. pag.

34. Letter of 12 August 1730, in *Letters of Defoe,* ed. Healey, 475–76.

Chapter Two

1. Ian Watt, *The Rise of the Novel: Studies in Defoe, Richardson, and Fielding* (Berkeley and Los Angeles: University of California Press, 1957), 35–36.

2. Peter Earle, *The World of Defoe* (London: Weidenfeld & Nicolson, 1976), viii.

3. *A True Collection of the Writings of the Author of the True Born English-man,* 2d ed. (London, 1705), sig. A4ᵛ.

4. Preface to *Jure Divino* (London, 1706), iii–iv.

5. *Review,* 29 July 1704, in *Defoe's Review,* 1:182.

6. James Sutherland, *Daniel Defoe: A Critical Study* (Cambridge, Mass.: Harvard University Press, 1971), 24.

7. *Review* 12 August 1704, in *Defoe's Review,* 1:197.

8. Cited in *Defoe: The Critical Heritage,* ed. Pat Rogers (London: Routledge & Kegan Paul, 1972), 38.

9. Cited in ibid., 39.

10. Henry L. Snyder, "Daniel Defoe, the Duchess of Marlborough, and the *Advice to the Electors of Great Britain,*" *Huntington Library Quarterly* 29 (November 1965):57.

11. *An Essay upon Projects* (1697); reissued as *Essays upon Several Projects: Effectual Ways for advancing the Interest of the Nation* (London, 1702), 1.

12. Ibid., 7–8.

13. *Augusta Triumphans,* in *Selected Poetry and Prose,* ed. Shugrue, 311–12.

14. *The Two Great Questions Consider'd* (London, 1700), 15.

15. Ibid., 26.

16. *Review,* 19 April 1709, in *Defoe's Review,* 6:26.

17. *Review,* 4 July 1704, in ibid., 1:153.

18. *Review,* 29 August 1704, in ibid., 1:217.

19. *Review,* 24 June 1710, in ibid., 7:149, 150.

20. Ibid., 150.

21. "The Preface," in *Review,* (London, 1705), vol. 1, sig. A$_2$.

22. "The Preface," in *Review,* (London, 1710), vol. 6, sig. A$_1$.

23. *Review,* 25 May 1710, in *Defoe's Review,* 7:97–98.

24. *Review,* 1 November 1709, in ibid., 6:358.

25. *Review,* 21 July 1705, in ibid., 2:238.

26. Sutherland, *Daniel Defoe,* 55.

27. *Reasons Why This Nation . . .,* in *The Versatile Defoe: An Anthology of Uncollected Writings by Daniel Defoe,* ed. Laura Ann Curtis (Totowa, N. J.: Rowman & Littlefield, 1979), 100.

28. Ibid., 102.

29. *A Seasonable Warning and Caution . . .,* in *Novels and Miscellaneous Works,* 12 vols. (London, 1856), 6:471.

30. Ibid., 468, 477.

31. *An Answer to a Question . . .,* in ibid., 481, 481–82.

32. Ibid., 488.

33. *Reasons against the Succession . . .,* in ibid., 508.

34. Ibid., 514–15.

35. Earle, *World of Defoe,* 93.

36. *And What If the Pretender Should Come?,* in *Novels and Miscellaneous Works* 6:538.

37. Ibid., 534.

38. Letter of 1713, in *Letters of Defoe,* ed. Healey, 407.

39. Lord Chief Justice Parker to Lord Bolingbroke, 15 April 1713, in ibid., 410–11, n.

40. *Review,* 11 August 1705, in *Defoe's Review,* 2:277.

41. *The Present State of the Parties In Great Britain* (1712), 24. Cited in Sutherland, *Daniel Defoe,* 45.

42. *Shortest Way*, in *Selected Poetry and Prose*, ed. Shugrue, 110. The first line is a biblical quotation, Song of Solomon 8:8.

43. *Shortest Way*, in *Selected Poetry and Prose*, ed. Shugrue, 111.

44. Ibid., 112.

45. Letter of 26 November 1706, in *Letters of Defoe*, ed. Healey, 158–59.

46. *Review*, 16 December 1710, in *Defoe's Review*, 7:453.

47. *Applebee's Original Weekly Journal*, 21 July 1722, in Lee, *Daniel Defoe*, 3:29.

Chapter Three

1. *Applebee's Original Weekly Journal*, 17 March 1722, in Lee, *Daniel Defoe*, 2:500.

2. *Review*, 28 February 1712, in *Defoe's Review*, 8:585.

3. *Review*, 2 July 1706, in ibid., 3:313, 314.

4. *Review*, 9 July 1706, in ibid., 3:327.

5. *Review*, 19 May 1711, in ibid., 8:94, 95.

6. Rodney M. Baine, *Daniel Defoe and the Supernatural* (Athens: University of Georgia Press, 1968), 13.

7. *Applebee's Original Weekly Journal*, 2 November 1723, 7 December 1723, in Lee, *Daniel Defoe*, 3:200, 212.

8. Keith Thomas, *Religion and the Decline of Magic* (New York: Charles Scribner's Sons, 1971), 452.

9. *The Political History of the Devil, as Well Ancient as Modern* (London, 1726), 345, 315.

10. *A System of Magick; or, A History of the Black Art. Being an Historical Account of Mankind's most early Dealing with the Devil; and how the Acquaintance on both Sides first began* (London, 1727), 378.

11. *An Essay on the History and Reality of Apparitions. Being An Account of what they are, and what they are not; whence they came, and whence they came not. As also How we may distinguish between the Apparitions of Good and Evil Spirits, and how we ought to Behave to them. With a great Variety of Surprizing and Diverting Examples, never Publish'd before* (London, 1727), 218, 28.

12. *Political History of the Devil*, 206, 204, 235.

13. *History and Reality of Apparitions*, 2, 100.

14. Ibid., 202.

15. Ibid., 320.

16. *The Complete English Tradesman: Directing him in the several Parts and Progressions of Trade* (1725–27), 2 vols., 3d. ed. (London, 1732), 1:308. For a modern analysis, see Lawrence Stone, "Social Mobility in England, 1500–1700," *Past and Present* 33 (April 1966):51–52.

17. *Review*, 22 January 1709, in *Defoe's Review*, 5:515.

18. *Review,* 25 June 1709, in ibid., 6:141–42.

19. *Review,* 27 May 1712, in ibid., 8:739.

20. *Review,* 22 January 1706, in ibid., 3:37, 38.

21. *Review,* 16 October 1707, in ibid., 4:423, 424.

22. *Complete English Tradesman,* 2:108, 111–12.

23. *The Poor Man's Plea,* in *Novels and Selected Writings,* 13:7.

24. *Review,* 26 December 1704, in *Defoe's Review,* 1:353, 354.

25. *Giving Alms no Charity,* in *The Genuine Works of Mr. Daniel D'Foe, Author of the True-born English-Man,* 2 vols. (London, 1710), 2:445.

26. Ibid., 448, 430.

27. Ibid., 437.

28. Ibid., 439.

29. *The Villainy of Stock-Jobbers Detected* (London, 1701), 19.

30. *A Brief State of the Inland or Home Trade of England,* in *The Versatile Defoe,* ed. Curtis, 213.

31. *Review,* 3 January 1706, in *Defoe's Review,* 3:6.

32. *Review,* 3 February 1713, in ibid., 9:107, 108.

33. Maximillian E. Novak, *Economics and the Fiction of Daniel Defoe* (Berkeley and Los Angeles: University of California Press, 1962), 5–6.

34. *The Villainy of Stock-Jobbers Detected,* 22, 25.

35. *Review,* 2 December 1708, in *Defoe's Review,* 5:426, 427.

36. *The Great Law of Subordination Consider'd* (London, 1724), 17.

37. *Every-Body's Business is No-Body's Business* (London, 1725), 4, 6.

38. *Great Law of Subordination,* 261.

39. *Review,* 31 January 1713, in *Defoe's Review,* 9:105–6.

40. *The Family Instructor,* in *The Novels and Miscellaneous Works of Daniel Defoe,* 20 vols. (1840–41; reprint ed., New York: AMS Press, 1973), 15:65–66.

41. Ibid., 135–36.

42. Ibid., 163.

43. Lawrence Stone, *The Family, Sex and Marriage in England 1500–1800* (New York: Harper & Row, 1979), 156.

Chapter Four

1. Watt, *Rise of the Novel,* 32, 24.

2. *Robinson Crusoe Examin'd and Criticis'd or A New Edition of Charles Gildon's Famous Pamphlet,* ed. Paul Dottin (London: J. M. Dent & Sons, 1923), 71–72.

3. "Appendix: Alexander Selkirk," in *Robinson Crusoe,* ed. Angus Ross (Harmondsworth, England: Penguin, 1965), 304, 306. All further references in the text are to this edition.

4. *The Englishman,* December 1713, reprinted in *Robinson Crusoe,* ed. Ross, 308.

5. J. Paul Hunter, *The Reluctant Pilgrim: Defoe's Emblematic Method and Quest for Form in "Robinson Crusoe"* (Baltimore: Johns Hopkins University Press, 1966), 19, 142.

6. G. A. Starr, *Defoe and Spiritual Autobiography* (Princeton: Princeton University Press, 1965), 72.

7. Pat Rogers, *Robinson Crusoe* (London: Allen & Unwin, 1979), 123, 124.

8. Watt, *Rise of the Novel,* 15.

9. Michael Seidel, *Epic Geography: James Joyce's "Ulysses"* (Princeton: Princeton University Press, 1976), 98–99.

10. Watt, *Rise of the Novel,* 65.

11. G. A. Starr, "Defoe's Prose Style: 1. The Language of Interpretation," *Modern Philology* 71 (1974):280, 287, 281.

12. James Joyce, "Daniel Defoe," ed. (from Italian manuscripts) and trans. Joseph Prescott, *Buffalo Studies* 1 (December 1964):24–25.

13. *The Farther Adventures of Robinson Crusoe; Being the Second and Last Part* (London, 1719), 299.

14. Manuel Schonhorn, Introduction to *A General History of the Robberies and Murders of the most notorious Pyrates, and also Their Policies, Discipline and Government* by Daniel Defoe (London: J. M. Dent & Sons, 1972), xxii. All further references in the text are to this edition.

15. Schonhorn, Introduction to *Pyrates,* xxii.

16. *Review,* 18 October 1707, in *Defoe's Review,* 4: 425.

17. See Maximillian E. Novak's introduction to "Of Captain Misson," *Augustan Reprint Society,* no. 87 (Los Angeles: University of California, William Andrews Clark Memorial Library, 1961), i.

18. *The Life, Adventures and Piracies of the Famous Captain Singleton,* intro. by James Sutherland (London: J. M. Dent & Sons, 1963), 4. All further references in the text are to this edition.

19. Manuel Schonhorn, "Defoe's *Captain Singleton:* A Reassessment with Observations," *Papers on Language and Literature* 7 (1971):45, 47.

Chapter Five

1. Paul Zweig, *The Adventurer* (London: J. M. Dent & Sons, 1974), 113, 114.

2. For a history of the picaresque, see Richard Bjornson, *The Picaresque Hero in European Fiction* (Madison: University of Wisconsin Press, 1977). For a discussion of Defoe's version of picaresque, see Robert Alter, *Rogue's Progress* (Cambridge, Mass.: Harvard University Press, 1964).

3. Maximillian E. Novak, *Realism, Myth, and History in Defoe's Fiction* (Lincoln: University of Nebraska Press, 1983), 123.

4. Moore, *Daniel Defoe,* 269.

5. *The History and Remarkable life of . . . Col. Jacque, Commonly Call'd Col. Jack,* ed. Samuel Holt Monk (London: Oxford University Press, 1970), 3, 4. All further references in the text are to this edition.

6. Bernard Mandeville, "An Essay on Charity Schools," in *The Fable of the Bees: or, Private Vices, Publick Benefits,* ed. F. B. Kaye, 2 vols. (Oxford: Clarendon Press, 1924), 1:268.

7. Ibid., 271, 272.

8. *Compleat English Gentleman,* 18.

9. David Blewett, *Defoe's Art of Fiction* (Toronto: University of Toronto Press, 1979), 94.

10. See above, chapter 1.

11. Everett Zimmerman, *Defoe and the Novel* (Berkeley and Los Angeles: University of California Press, 1975), 2.

12. Watt, *Rise of the Novel,* 100.

13. Novak, *Realism, Myth, and History,* 77.

14. *The Life and Actions of Jonathan Wild,* in *Romances and Narratives by Daniel Defoe,* ed. George A. Aitken, 16 vols. (London: J. M. Dent & Co., 1895), 16:256.

15. *Moll Flanders,* ed. G. A. Starr (New York: Oxford University Press, 1981), 214. All further references in the text are to this edition.

16. *The History of the remarkable Life of John Sheppard,* in *Novels and Selected Writings,* 2:166. All further references in the text are to this edition.

17. Watt, *Rise of the Novel,* 117.

18. Starr, *Defoe and Spiritual Autobiography,* 127.

19. Leo Braudy, "Daniel Defoe and the Anxieties of Autobiography," *Genre* 6 (1973):76.

20. Lois A. Chaber, "Matriarchal Mirror: Women and Capital in *Moll Flanders,*" *PMLA* 97 (March 1982):223.

21. *Conjugal Lewdness,* intro. by Maximillian E. Novak (Gainesville, Fl.: Scholars' Facsimilies and Reprints, 1967), 217, 96.

Chapter Six

1. Novak, *Realism, Myth, and History,* 99.

2. Ian Bell, *Defoe's Fiction* (London: Croom Helm, 1985), 154–57.

3. David Blewett, Introduction, to *Roxana* (Harmondsworth, England: Penguin, 1982), 11–13. All further references in the text are to this edition.

4. Rodney M. Baine, "*Roxana's* Georgian Setting," *Studies in English Literature* 15 (1974):459–73; and Paul Alkon, *Defoe and Fictional Time* (Athens: University of Georgia Press, 1979), 53–58.

5. Blewett, Introduction to *Roxana,* 13.

6. Starr, *Defoe and Spiritual Autobiography,* 165.

7. Blewett, Introduction to *Roxana,* 390.

8. *Conjugal Lewdness,* 26.

9. *An Essay upon Projects* (1697); reissued as *Essays upon Several Projects: Effectual Ways for advancing the Interest of the Nation* (London: 1702), 284.

10. *Conjugal Lewdness,* 103.

11. Blewett, Introduction to *Roxana,* 393.

12. G. A. Starr, *Defoe and Casuistry* (Princeton: Princeton University Press, 1971), vii.

13. E. Anthony James, *Daniel Defoe's Many Voices: A Rhetorical Study of Prose Style and Literary Method* (Amsterdam: Rodopi NV, 1972), 236.

14. As David Blewett points out, "Roxana" in Defoe's day had become a name associated with wicked female ambition of an oriental sort. Introduction to *Roxana,* 394.

15. Michael M. Boardman, *Defoe and the Uses of Narrative* (New Brunswick, N. J.: Rutgers University Press, 1983), 140.

16. Ibid., 140–41.

Chapter Seven

1. James, *Daniel Defoe's Many Voices,* 321.

2. *A True Relation of the Apparition of one Mrs. Veal . . .,* in *Romances and Narratives of Daniel Defoe,* ed. George A. Aitken, 16 vols. (London: J. M. Dent & Co., 1895), 15:232, 234.

3. Ibid., 225.

4. *The Storm* (London, 1704), sig. A7ᵛ, p. 11.

5. *Ibid.,* 70.

6. *Serious Reflections During the Life . . . of Robinson Crusoe* (London, 1720), 216, 211, 225.

7. Hunter, *Reluctant Pilgrim,* 204.

8. Paul Korshin, *Typologies in England 1650–1820* (Princeton: Princeton University Press, 1982), 224, 223.

9. Alkon, *Defoe and Fictional Time,* 230.

10. Zimmerman, *Defoe and the Novel,* 109.

11. *A Journal of the Plague Year,* ed. Anthony Burgess and Christopher Bristow (Harmondsworth, England: Penguin, 1966), 209. All further references in the text are to this edition.

12. *Serious Reflections,* 221.

13. Zimmerman, *Defoe and the Novel,* 111.

14. Manuel Schonhorn, "Defoe's *Journal of the Plague Year:* Topography and Intention," *Review of English Studies,* n. s. 19 (1968):397.

15. Novak, *Realism, Myth, and History,* 53.

16. *Memoirs of a Cavalier,* ed. James T. Boulton (London: Oxford University Press, 1972), 44. All further references in the text are to this edition.

17. William Minto, *Daniel Defoe* (London: Macmillan, 1887), 169.

18. *A Tour through the Whole Island of Great Britain,* 1:3. All further references are indicated parenthetically in the text.

19. F. Bastian, "Defoe's Tour and the Historian," *History Today* 17 (1967):847, 849.

20. *Augusta Triumphans,* in *Selected Poetry and Prose,* ed. Shugrue, 314.

21. Pat Rogers, "Literary Art in Defoe's *Tour:* The Rhetoric of Growth and Decay," *Eighteenth-Century Studies* 6 (1972–73):155–56.

Selected Bibliography

PRIMARY SOURCES

1. Collections

There is no standard, collected edition of Defoe's works. John Robert Moore, *A Checklist of the Writings of Daniel Defoe,* 2d. ed. (Bloomington: University of Indiana Press, 1960; reprint ed., Hamden, Conn.: Archon Books, 1971) lists over five hundred titles, and all but a few have been reproduced by University Microfilms. The following is a list of partial collections of Defoe's works, mostly the major narratives and some of the social and economic writings, some one-volume modern anthologies of his nonfictional writings, and significant modern editions of his novels.

Novels and Miscellaneous Works. 20 vols. 1840–41. Reprint. New York: AMS Press, 1973.

Novels and Miscellaneous Works. 12 vols. London: Bohn's British Classics, 1856.

Romances and Narratives of Daniel Defoe. 16 vols. Edited by George A. Aitken. London: J. M. Dent & Co., 1895.

Novels and Selected Writings. 14 vols. 1927–28. Reprint. (in 9 vols). Totowa, N. J.: Rowman & Littlefield, 1974. This is the best modern collected edition.

The Letters of Daniel Defoe. Edited by George Harris Healey. Oxford: Clarendon Press, 1955.

Defoe's Review. 22 vols. Edited by Arthur Wellesley Secord. 1938. Reprint. New York: AMS Press, 1965.

Boulton, James T., ed. *Selected Writings of Daniel Defoe.* Cambridge: Cambridge University Press, 1975.

Curtis, Laura, ed. *The Versatile Defoe: An Anthology of Uncollected Writings by Daniel Defoe.* Totowa, N. J.: Rowman & Littlefield, 1979.

Lee, William. *Daniel Defoe: His Life, and Recently Discovered Writings.* 3 vols. 1869. Reprint. New York: Burt Franklin, 1969. Reprints some of Defoe's contributions to periodicals other than the *Review.*

Shugrue, Michael F., ed. *Selected Poetry and Prose of Daniel Defoe.* New York: Holt, Rinehart & Winston, 1968.

2. Novels and Other Single Works of Defoe

Captain Singleton. Edited by James Sutherland. London: J. M. Dent & Sons, 1963.

Captain Singleton. Edited by Shiv K. Kumar. London: Oxford University Press, 1969.

Colonel Jack. Edited by Samuel Holt Monk. London: Oxford University Press, 1970.

A General History of the Pyrates. Edited by Manuel Schonhorn. London: J. M. Dent & Sons, 1972.

A Journal of the Plague Year. Edited by Anthony Burgess and Christopher Bristow. Harmondsworth, England: Penguin, 1966.

A Journal of the Plague Year. Edited by Louis Landa. London: Oxford University Press, 1969.

Memoirs of a Cavalier. Edited by James T. Boulton. London: Oxford University Press, 1972.

Moll Flanders. Edited by J. Paul Hunter. New York: Crowell, 1970.

Moll Flanders. Edited by G. A. Starr. 1971. Reprint. New York: Oxford University Press, 1984.

Robinson Crusoe: An Authoritative Text, Backgrounds and Sources, Criticism. Edited by Michael Shinagel. New York: Norton, 1975.

Robinson Crusoe. Edited by Angus Ross. Harmondsworth, England: Penguin, 1965.

Roxana. Edited by Jane Jack. London: Oxford University Press, 1969.

Roxana. Edited by David Blewett. Harmondsworth, England: Penguin, 1982.

A Tour through the Whole Island of Great Britain. 2 vols. Introductions by G. D. H. Cole and D. C. Browning. London: J. M. Dent & Sons, 1962.

A Tour through the Whole Island of Great Britain. Abridged and edited by Pat Rogers. Harmondsworth, England: Penguin, 1971.

SECONDARY SOURCES

1. Bibliographies

Novak, Maximillian E. "Daniel Defoe." In *The New Cambridge Bibliography of English Literature,* edited by George Watson, 2:880–917. Cambridge: Cambridge University Press, 1971.

————. "Defoe." In *The English Novel: Select Bibliographical Guides,* edited by A. E. Dyson. London: Oxford University Press, 1974. Evaluates Defoe criticism and lists 150 works by and about Defoe.

Stoler, John A. *Daniel Defoe: An Annotated Bibliography of Modern Criticism, 1900–1980.* New York: Garland Press, 1984. Comprehensive, fully annotated list that includes editions of Defoe's works and books and articles about them.

2. Books

Alkon, Paul. *Defoe and Fictional Time.* Athens: University of Georgia Press, 1979. Critically sophisticated reading of Defoe's manipulations of time in his novels.

Backscheider, Paula. *A Being More Intense.* New York: AMS Press, 1984. Places Defoe's narratives in a line of autobiographical narrative that begins with Bunyan.

————. *Daniel Defoe: Ambition and Innovation.* Lexington: University of Kentucky Press, 1986. Comprehensive discussion of all of Defoe's literary career.

Baine, Rodney M. *Daniel Defoe and the Supernatural.* Athens: University of Georgia Press, 1968. Discussion of the importance in his work of Defoe's belief in the supernatural.

Bastian, F. *Defoe's Early Life.* Totowa, N. J.: Barnes & Noble, 1981. Exhaustive biographical discussion of Defoe's early years.

Bell, Ian. *Defoe's Fiction.* London: Croom Helm, 1985. Original treatment of the fiction in the context of popular narrative in the early eighteenth century.

Birdsall, Virginia Ogden. *Defoe's Perpetual Seekers: A Study of the Major Fiction.* Lewisburg, Pa: Bucknell University Press, 1985. Reads the novels as crucially influenced by Defoe's reading of Hobbes and Rochester.

Blewett, David. *Defoe's Art of Fiction.* Toronto: University of Toronto Press, 1979. A reading of the major novels that explores their artistic and moral dimensions.

Boardman, Michael M. *Defoe and the Uses of Narrative.* New Brunswick, N. J.: Rutgers University Press, 1983. Perceptive discussion of the formal innovations of Defoe's novels.

Curtis, Laura. *The Elusive Daniel Defoe.* Totowa, N. J.: Vision Press and Barnes & Noble, 1984. Biographically based interpretation that sees Defoe as divided between truthfulness and manipulative fabrication.

Damrosch, Leopold. *God's Plot and Man's Stories.* Chicago: University of Chicago Press, 1985. Insightful discussion of Defoe's fiction, especially *Robinson Crusoe,* in Puritan tradition as exemplified by Milton and Bunyan.

Davis, Lennard. *Factual Fictions: The Origins of the English Novel.* New York: Columbia University Press, 1983. Stimulating account of the development of the novel in relation to changing uses of print and narrative.

Earle, Peter. *The World of Defoe.* London: Weidenfield & Nicolson, 1976. Informative survey of Defoe's works and ideas in relation to his times.

Hunter, J. Paul. *The Reluctant Pilgrim: Defoe's Emblematic Method and Quest for Form in "Robinson Crusoe."* Baltimore: Johns Hopkins University Press, 1966. Important study of *Robinson Crusoe* as the expression of Puritan world view.

James, E. Anthony. *Daniel Defoe's Many Voices: A Rhetorical Study of Prose Style and Literary Method.* Amsterdam: Rodopi NV, 1972. Extended analyses of Defoe's literary style and artistry.

McKillop, A. D. *The Early Masters of English Fiction.* Lawrence: University of Kansas Press, 1968. Informative history of the eighteenth-century novel.

Moore, John Robert. *Daniel Defoe: Citizen of the Modern World.* Chicago: University of Chicago Press, 1958. Fact-filled biographical and critical discussion.

Novak, Maximillian E. *Economics and the Fiction of Daniel Defoe.* Berkeley and Los Angeles: University of California Press, 1962. Most thorough modern analysis of Defoe's surprisingly conservative economic views.

————. *Defoe and the Nature of Man.* London: Oxford University Press, 1963. Places Defoe in the intellectual currents of his time and shows how his ideas are dramatized in his fiction.

————. *Realism, Myth, and History in Defoe's Fiction.* Lincoln: University of Nebraska Press, 1983. Explores the often underestimated complexities of Defoe's fiction.

Richetti, John J. *Popular Fiction before Richardson: Narrative Patterns 1700–1739.* Oxford: Clarendon Press, 1969. Places some of Defoe's narratives in the context of popular fiction.

————. *Defoe's Narratives: Situations and Structures.* Oxford: Clarendon Press, 1975. Readings of the novels as resolutions of cultural contradictions and expressions of individual will to power.

Secord, Arthur W. *Studies in the Narrative Method of Defoe.* University of Illinois Studies in Language and Literature, no. 9 (1924). Reprint. New York: Russell & Russell, 1963. Detailed tracing of Defoe's sources for his fictional narratives, especially *Robinson Crusoe* and *Captain Singleton.*

Shinagel, Michael. *Daniel Defoe and Middle-Class Gentility.* Cambridge, Mass.: Harvard University Press, 1968. Defoe's social aspirations as crucial theme in the fiction and some of the nonfiction.

Sill, Geoffrey. *Defoe and the Idea of Fiction, 1713–1719.* Newark: University of Delaware Press, 1983. Reads *Robinson Crusoe* as growing out of Defoe's early political writing.

Starr, G. A. *Defoe and Spiritual Autobiography.* Princeton: Princeton University Press, 1965. Finds the origin and organizing principle of Defoe's fiction in Puritan diaries.

————. *Defoe and Casuistry*. Princeton: Princeton University Press, 1971. Traces insightfully the influence of method of moral judgment for individual cases of conscience on structure of Defoe's fiction.

Sutherland, James. *Defoe*. London: Methuen, 1937. Most readable and sensible biography.

————. *Daniel Defoe: A Critical Study*. Cambridge, Mass.: Harvard University Press, 1971. A study in some depth of the nonfiction as well as the fiction.

Watt, Ian. *The Rise of the Novel: Studies in Defoe, Richardson, and Fielding*. Berkeley and Los Angeles: University of California Press, 1957. Important analysis of Defoe's achievement as pioneer of realistic novel.

Zimmerman, Everett. *Defoe and the Novel*. Berkeley and Los Angeles: University of California Press, 1975. Examines the changes in Defoe's moral and literary assumptions expressed in his novels.

3. Articles

Backscheider, Paula. "Defoe's Women: Snares and Prey." *Studies in Eighteenth-Century Culture* 5 (1976):103–20. Feminist survey of Defoe's depiction of women, especially Moll Flanders and Roxana.

Braudy, Leo. "Daniel Defoe and the Anxieties of Autobiography." *Genre* 6 (1973):76–97. Suggestive treatment of the novels as pioneering dramatizations of anxiety of personal identity.

Brown, Homer O. "The Displaced Self in the Novels of Daniel Defoe." *English Literary History* 38 (1971):562–90. Sees Defoe's fiction as confessions in which characters expose their lives and conceal their identities.

Byrd, Max, ed. *Daniel Defoe: A Collection of Critical Essays*. Englewood Cliffs, N. J.: Prentice-Hall, 1976. Influential critical essays, mainly on *Robinson Crusoe* and *Moll Flanders*.

Elliott, Robert C., ed. *Twentieth Century Interpretations of "Moll Flanders": A Collection of Critical Essays*. Englewood Cliffs, N. J.: Prentice-Hall, 1970. Gathers key essays on *Moll Flanders*.

Ellis, Frank H., ed. *Twentieth Century Interpretations of "Robinson Crusoe": A Collection of Critical Essays*. Englewood Cliffs, N. J.: Prentice-Hall, 1969. Some essays, some excerpts from books, and a valuable introduction by Ellis.

Rader, Ralph. "Defoe, Richardson, Joyce, and the Concept of Form in the Novel." In *Autobiography, Biography, and the Novel: Papers Read at a Clark Library Seminar*. Berkeley and Los Angeles: University of California Press, 1973. Using *Moll Flanders* as example, defines Defoe's novels as "simulated naive" autobiographies. Complex and insightful.

Starr, G. A. "Defoe's Prose Style: 1. The Language of Interpretation." *Modern Philology* 71 (1974):277–94. Finds that too much stress has been put on "objective" and factual nature of Defoe's style. Discusses it as rendering the subjectivity of experience.

Index